The Songwriter's Journal

Other Books Available From
STONY MEADOW PUBLISHING

Inspiration for Songwriters: Tips and Tricks to Unlocking the Muse
ISBN-13: 978-0-9787925-0-3 / ISBN-10: 0-9787925-0-5
by Stan Swanson

The Songwriter's Journal
52 Weeks of Songwriting Ideas and Inspiration

by
Stan Swanson

Stony Meadow Publishing
Denver, Colorado

Stony Meadow Publishing
Broomfield, Colorado

www.StonyMeadowPublishing.com

The Songwriter's Journal
52 Weeks of Songwriting Ideas and Inspirations
ISBN-13: 978-0-9787925-1-0
ISBN-10: 0-9787925-1-3

Printed in the United States of America

PUBLISHER'S NOTE:
This publication is designed to provide accurate and authoritative information in regard to the subject matter covered. It is sold with the understanding that the publisher and the author are not engaged in rendering legal, accounting, or other professional service. If legal advice or other expert assistant is required, the service of a competent professional person should be sought.

> *"Music is a higher revelation than all wisdom and philosophy.*
> *Music is the electrical soil in which the spirit lives, thinks and*
> *invents."* **-- Ludwig van Beethoven**

You hold in your hands the key to creating thousands of songs. Whether you use this book on a daily basis and follow it week by week for the course of a year or simply pick it up occasionally, it holds the power to inspire more ideas than anything other than your own mind.

I have written hundreds of songs over the years and while I have never had a hit single, it is the experience of writing those songs and working hard to improve my talent that allows me to convey that experience to you in book form.

The Songwriter's Journal: 52 Weeks of Songwriting Ideas and Inspiration is actually my second book on the subject. The first, ***Inspiration for Songwriters: Tips and Tricks to Unlocking the Muse***, is what led me to create another book on the same subject. Many readers told me they loved the first book, but thought that a "journal" type book would be even better. They wanted something they could not only use on a daily or weekly basis, but jot down notes or song titles or lyrics as well. It sounded like a great idea and so here it is . (Now I need all those people to go out and buy a copy.)

There is no correct way to use this book. You can use it as a daily journal and begin on the first page or you can jump around to different pages to find the inspiration you need. Whether you sit down on Sunday and write a complete song or simply jot down a song title or idea doesn't matter. The important thing is to use this book on a regular basis and fill its pages with scribbles and notes.

Hopefully you will find that at the end of a year you'll have filled the pages with all sorts of good stuff.

The first few pages show the basic design and layout of the book and explain the purpose of the information included within. After that, you are on your own. Let the book lead you, but allow the muse to slip in between the pages. After all, she always knows best.

-- Stan Swanson

SUNDAY

Use the first page in each section to jot down notes, song titles or ideas. Make sure you jot something down every day. Try to use this journal page as a source of inspiration. Refer back to these pages as you work on a new song or idea. You never know when something you jotted down three months ago might be a perfect fit for your newest composition. Of course, you can also use it as a calendar to jot down appointments and important dates.

SATURDAY

Songwriting Exercise

Go over to your bookshelf (you do own a book or two, don't you?) and choose a book at random. (It doesn't matter whether it's fiction or nonfiction.) Flip the book open to any page and poin... ...age. Your assignment is to write a ... ...sn't important. If you pointed to a se... ...t rid of them, don't let that stop you. ... *Pet Petunia* is just waiting to be written.

> Here are 52 great exercises to inspire your next song. Use one every week or select one at random.

Song Titles

- Still Amazed By Your Love
- I Like You Better I...
- Whistling in th...
- Dogs Just Barking A...
- Stories I've Never Told

> Song titles cannot be copyrighted. If any of these song titles inspire a new tune, go for it!

Chord Progression fo...
C-Am-C-G (I-vi-I...)

> Many songwriters begin the creative process with a simple chord progression. Give it a try!

Word Association Exercise

As Easy As _____

_____ Windows

A _____ In The Afternoon

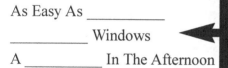

> These exercises can lead to new song titles, hooks or simply get you started on that next verse.

Songwriters Hall of Fame: Paul Simon

Hall of Fame Induction: 1982. Paul Simon has four #1 singles to his songwriting credits and had five albums listed in Rolling Stone's "500 Greatest Albums of All Time." He ... of Fame as a member of Simon an... 2001. He has won 12 Grammys a... special. **Little known fact:** Simo... Carole King in the 1960's as a duo called *The Cosines*. **Recommended listening:** *Bookends* and *Bridge Over Troubled Water* with Art Garfunkel as well as *There Goes Rhymin' Simon* and *Graceland*.

> Nothing can inspire you more to write a new song than listening to a good songwriter or a great album.

"Twenty years from ... ings you didn't do than b... nes. Sail away from the s... ails. Explore. Dream. Dis...

> Looking for inspiration or motivation to get that muse flowing? Take a look at an inspirational quote.

Inspirational Quote

An Idea to Write a Song

It is 1865. You are riding [hidden] ...hen you realize your canteen is dry [hidden] in sight. And then your horse dies...

> Sometimes just finding the seed of an idea for a song is the toughest. Use these whenever you feel stuck.

Note Sequence for a [hidden]
G-B-A-B-D-C-B-A

> Play these notes on your guitar or keyboard. Vary the note length and see what melody pops up.

Power Words

Lantern / Crumble / [hidden]

> Use power words when writing your next song. They are strong words that demand a listener's attention.

Cliches, Expressions, Slang and Idioms

- I love being free, it's the bes[hidden]
- The more things chang[hidden]
- It wouldn't be fun if life wa[hidden]

> Don't rely on cliches too much, but they are great for inspiring song titles, hooks and introductory lines.

Rolling Stone Magazine's Greatest Songs of all Time -- #1

LIKE A ROLLING STONE (Bob Dylan) 1965

A FEW LINES: "You said you'd never compromise. / With the mystery tramp but now you [hidden] u stare into the vacuum of his ey[hidden] DID YOU KN[hidden] this was a big breakthrough when [hidden] a hit. Most stations at that time refused to play songs much longer than 3 minutes.

> Listening to great songwriters can improve your own songwriting. Try to emulate the things they do.

Songwriter's Toolkit

Band in a Box (PG Music)

CD-ROM Software for Windows 98 / XP / Me / 2000 / Mac Band-In-A-Box 2006 makes [hidden] e the best in riffs and rolls by si[hidden] stan- dard chord symbols (like C, F[hidden] style, then add a complete professio[hidden] rums, guitar and strings in Jazz, Pop, Country, Classical and more. List: $88.00.
www.pgmusic.com

> A songwriter is not equipped to create at his best without a few tools of the trade. Here are some great ones.

Songwriter Quote

"I consider mys[hidden] like a poet and I'll die [hidden]

> Who knows more about songwriting than the songwriters themselves. They can inspire as well as enlighten.

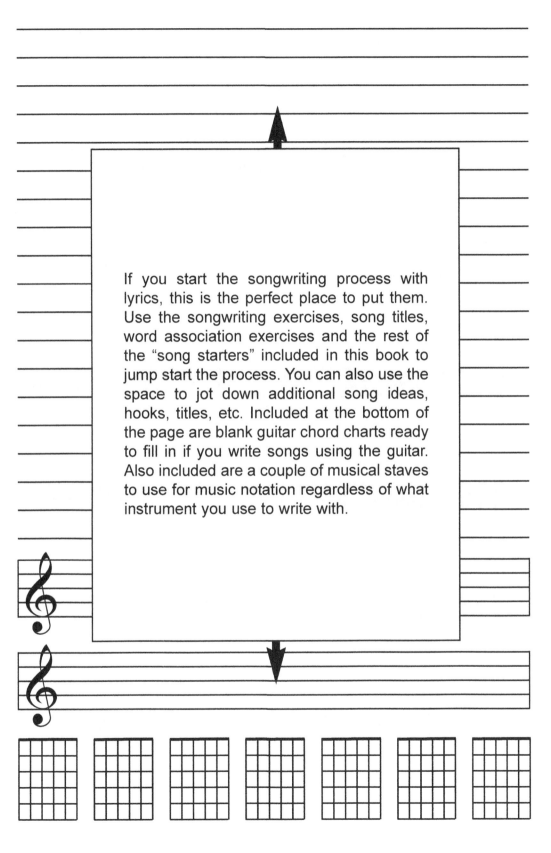

If you start the songwriting process with lyrics, this is the perfect place to put them. Use the songwriting exercises, song titles, word association exercises and the rest of the "song starters" included in this book to jump start the process. You can also use the space to jot down additional song ideas, hooks, titles, etc. Included at the bottom of the page are blank guitar chord charts ready to fill in if you write songs using the guitar. Also included are a couple of musical staves to use for music notation regardless of what instrument you use to write with.

SUNDAY

MONDAY

TUESDAY

WEDNESDAY

THURSDAY

FRIDAY

SATURDAY

Songwriting Exercise

Go over to your bookshelf (you do own a book or two, don't you?) and choose a book at random. (It doesn't matter whether it's fiction or nonfiction.) Flip the book open to any page and point your finger at a line on the page. Your assignment is to write a song about that line. The subject matter isn't important. If you pointed to a sentence about garden insects and how to get rid of them, don't let that stop you. *The Night the Yellow Woollybears Ate My Pet Petunia* is just waiting to be written.

Song Titles

- Still Amazed By Your Love
- I Like You Better In An Alternate Reality
- Whistling In The Graveyard
- Dogs Just Barking At The Man In The Moon
- Stories I've Never Told

Chord Progression for a Song
C-Am-C-G (I-vi-I-V)

Word Association Exercise

As Easy As _____   Return to _____

_____ Windows   Songs Of The _____

A _____ In The Afternoon   Jealousy And _____

Songwriters Hall of Fame: Paul Simon

Hall of Fame Induction: 1982. Paul Simon has four #1 singles to his songwriting credits and five albums listed in *Rolling Stone* magazine's *500 Greatest Albums of All Time*. He was inducted into the Rock and Roll Hall of Fame as a member of Simon and Garfunkel in 1990 and as a solo artist in 2001. He has won 12 Grammys as well as an Emmy for a televised concert special. **Little known fact:** Simon recorded several unreleased demos with Carole King in the 1960's as a duo called *The Cosines*. **Recommended listening:** *Bookends* and *Bridge Over Troubled Water* with Art Garfunkel as well as *There Goes Rhymin' Simon* and *Graceland* as a solo artist.

"Twenty years from now you will be more disappointed by the things you didn't do than by the ones you did do. So throw off the bowlines. Sail away from the safe harbor. Catch the trade winds in your sails. Explore. Dream. Discover." -- **Mark Twain**

Inspirational Quote

An Idea to Write a Song About

It is 1865. You are riding across a desert in the American southwest when you realize your canteen is dry as a bone. You are lost without a landmark in sight. And then your horse dies...

Note Sequence for a Song
G-B-A-B-D-C-B-A

Power Words

Lantern / Crumble / Mystery / Tangle / Carnivorous

Cliches, Expressions, Slang and Idioms
- I love being free, it's the best way to be
- The more things change, the more they stay the same
- It wouldn't be fun if life was easy

Rolling Stone Magazine's Greatest Songs of all Time -- #1
LIKE A ROLLING STONE (Bob Dylan) 1965

A FEW LINES: "You said you'd never compromise. / With the mystery tramp but now you realize. / He's not selling any alibis. / As you stare into the vacuum of his eyes. / And say do you want to make a deal?"

DID YOU KNOW... At just over six minutes in length, this was a big breakthrough when the song received radio play and became a hit. Most stations at that time refused to play songs much longer than 3 minutes.

Songwriter's Toolkit
Band in a Box (PG Music)

CD-ROM Software for Windows 98 / XP / Me / 2000 / Mac

Band-In-A-Box makes composing your own songs easy. Create the best in riffs and rolls by simply typing in the chords for any song using standard chord symbols (like C, Fm7 or C13b9). Choose your favorite song style, then add a complete professional quality arrangement of piano, bass, drums, guitar and strings in Jazz, Pop, Country, Classical and more. ($99.00)

www.pgmusic.com

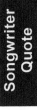

*"I consider myself a poet first and a musician second. I live like a poet and I'll die like a poet." -- **Bob Dylan***

The Songwriter's Journal: WEEK 2

SUNDAY

MONDAY

TUESDAY

WEDNESDAY

THURSDAY

FRIDAY

SATURDAY

Songwriting Exercise

Find a CD you enjoy and choose one song. Take the melody of the song and write new words to it. This is a great exercise for new writers and it can also get established songwriters out of the rut. The exercise teaches song structure and strengthens your lyric writing at the same time. Step two of this exercise is to take your original lyrics and write a new melody to them. Make sure it differs from the song you used as your template. Once you have finished both steps of this exercise, you will have written a new, original song.

Song Titles

- A Wrinkle In The Mind
- Hope Stands Waiting
- Thirteen Fish In A Ten Fish Bowl
- Tigers Made Of Tin
- Sassafras Tea

Chord Progression for a Song
C-G-Fm-C (I-V-iv-I)

Word Association Exercises

Like A Wall Of _____   A Little Bit Of _____

Big _____ , Little _____   Float Like A _____

_____ And Villains   First _____ , Last _____

Songwriters Hall of Fame: Chuck Berry

Hall of Fame Induction: 1986. Chuck Berry was among the first groups of inductees into the Songwriter's Hall of Fame. Although he only has one #1 single to his name, he is considered one of the chief pioneers of the rock era. (He also had several R&B hit singles.) In 2004, six of his songs were included in the Rolling Stone magazines 500 Greatest Songs of All Time list. **Little known fact:** The Beach Boys' *Surfin' U.S.A.* so closely resembled Berry's *Sweet Little Sixteen* that the threat of a lawsuit gave Berry a cowriting credit. **Recommended listening:** *The Great Twenty-Eight, The London Chuck Berry Sessions* and *Anthology.*

"A musician must make music, an artist must paint, a poet must write, if he is to be ultimately at peace with himself. What one can be, one must be." -- **Abraham Maslow**"

Inspirational Quote

An Idea to Write a Song About
You are a young child swinging merrily on a swing set in the park. You look around and suddenly stop swinging as you realize you don't see your mother or father. And it's getting dark...

Note Sequence for a Song
F-C-B-C-B-A-B-C

Power Words
Fog / Castle / Monk / Stampede / Antique

Cliches, Expressions, Slang and Idioms
- Colder than a Klondike Bar
- The devil you know is better than the devil you don't
- Like death warmed over

Rolling Stone Magazine's Greatest Songs of all Time -- #2
SATISFACTION (The Rolling Stones) 1965
(Songwriters: Jagger/Richards)
A FEW LINES: "When I'm drivin' in my car. / And a man comes on the radio. / And he's tellin' me more and more. / About some useless information. / Supposed to fire my imagination. / I can't get no, no, no."
DID YOU KNOW... Keith Richards woke up in his hotel room during the Stones 3rd U.S. tour with the guitar riff and lyric "can't get no satisfaction" in his head. He recorded it on a portable tape deck, then went back to sleep. The tape contained his guitar riff followed by the sounds of him snoring.

Songwriter's Toolkit
The Beatles Best: Over 120 Great Beatles Hits (Piano, Vocal, Guitar)
Hal Leonard Publishing (ISBN: 0881885983)
This one is great no matter what type of music you enjoy. Complete with piano and vocal arrangements as well as guitar chords, it includes 124 of the Beatles greatest hits. The songbook encompasses a wide variety of Beatles' songs including *All My Loving, Come Together, Eleanor Rigby, Get Back, Help!, Hey Jude, Let It Be, Michelle* and many more. ($32.95)

Songwriter Quote

Music is your own experience, your own thoughts, your wisdom. If you don't live it, it won't come out of your horn. They teach you there's a boundary line to music. But, man, there's no boundary line to art." -- Charlie Parker

SUNDAY

MONDAY

TUESDAY

WEDNESDAY

THURSDAY

FRIDAY

SATURDAY

Songwriting Exercise

This exercise is called "freeform association." You may be familiar with this from an English or creative writing class, but it works great for writing songs as well. Take out a pen and paper and begin writing down words as they come to you. Throw in some good nouns, verbs and adjectives. (Try and make many of these "power words.") Once you have scribbled down a couple of dozen words, take your pen and connect 3 or 4 of them in a logical sequence. More often than not, you'll find a new song title, hook or idea.

Song Titles

- Letters Written In Haste
- The Cows Came Home (But They Wouldn't Go To Bed)
- Too Many Birthday Cards
- Don't Bother To Knock ('Cause I Ain't Home)
- Kisses Like Chocolate

Chord Progression for a Song
Am-C-G (i-III-VII)

Word Association Exercises

Lost In _____

Shocked By The _____

Last Bus To _____

Dancing Like A _____

_____ Like A Dream

Heaven Is _____

Songwriters Hall of Fame: Joni Mitchell

Hall of Fame Induction: 1997. Although Mitchell spent much of her youth longing to be an artist, her talents as a songwriter led her down another path. Her songwriting career reached its highest visibility when Judy Collins had a top-ten hit in 1968 with *Both Sides Now.* Known for her open tuning styles, Rolling Stone Magazine named her the 72nd Greatest Guitarist in their 2003 list. She was the highest-ranked woman on the list. **Little known fact:** Mitchell has, through photography or painting, created the artwork for each of her albums and has described herself as a "painter derailed by circumstance." **Recommended listening:** *Blue, Ladies of the Canyon* and *Court and Spark.*

"To reach a port we must sail, sometimes with the wind and sometimes against it. But we must not drift or lie at anchor." -- Oliver Wendell Holmes

Inspirational Quote

An Idea to Write a Song About

You're a turkey. (A "real" turkey, not the people kind of turkey.) You're strutting around the farmyard feeling pretty good about life. Then you hear the farmer say something about "thanksgiving" and get a very strange feeling...

Note Sequence for a Song
F-F-A-F-F-G

Power Words
Cloudburst / Wizard / Brass / Jingle / Crackle

Cliches, Expressions, Slang and Idioms
- Counting on my good fortune
- Like rats abandoning a sinking ship
- Receive your just rewards

Rolling Stone Magazine's Greatest Songs of all Time -- #3
IMAGINE (John Lennon) 1971 (Songwriter: Lennon)
A FEW LINES: "Imagine no possessions. / I wonder if you can. / No need for greed or hunger. / A brotherhood of man. / Imagine all the people. / Sharing all the world."
DID YOU KNOW... A sidewalk mosaic in a section of Central Park dedicated to Lennon spells out the word "Imagine." The area is called "Strawberry Fields" and is located across from the apartment building where he was shot.

Songwriter's Toolkit
Oxford Rhyming Dictionary (Oxford University Press)
by Clive Upton (ISBN: 0192801155)
This might be the ultimate rhymer's companion. It is an ideal reference tool for songwriters as it offers over 85,000 words and a solid chance of finding even the most elusive rhyme. It is simple and straight forward. Words are organized according to their sound rather than alphabetically, which means you can find a rhyme to match a word as it is spoken, rather than how it is spelled. The book also contains near rhymes, close rhymes and half rhymes. ($40.00)

Songwriter Quote

"Too many pieces of music finish too long after the end."
-- Igor Stravinsky

The Songwriter's Journal: WEEK 4

SUNDAY

MONDAY

TUESDAY

WEDNESDAY

THURSDAY

FRIDAY

SATURDAY

Songwriting Exercise

This exercise requires only your imagination. Sit back in a quiet place and think back on your childhood. Once a particular incident creeps in, focus only on that particular time in your life. Try and remember what the setting and the weather was like. Was it snowing? Do you remember the smell of fresh cut grass? Were other people around? Why did this particular childhood "event" stick in your mind? Once you have given it sufficient meditation, put your thoughts to paper and then into song.

Song Titles

- It's All Over (Again)
- Friends I Could Live Without
- Casting Lines In Shallow Water
- Claptrap Cadillac
- Kalidescopic Laughter

Chord Progression for a Song
   C-Am-G-F (I-vi-V-IV)

Word Association Exercises

_____ And Yesterday   _____ And Feathers

When _____ Strikes   Somewhere In _____

Child Of The _____   Copper And _____

Songwriters Hall of Fame: Kris Kristofferson

Hall of Fame Induction: 1985. Kristofferson spent many years honing his songwriting talents and paying his dues before finally achieving the success he had sought for so long. He was initially known more for his country hits (*Jody and the Kid* from Roy Drusky and *Sunday Mornin' Comin' Down* from Ray Stevens) until Janis Joplin's cover of *Me and Bobby McGee* in 1971. He has also appeared in more than 15 movies. **Little known fact:** Kristofferson joined with Johnny Cash, Waylon Jennings and Willie Nelson to form the supergroup *The Highwaymen* in 1985. **Recommended listening:** *The Silver Tongued Devil and I, Singer/Songwriter* and *Repossessed.*

"Challenges make you discover things about yourself that you never really knew. They're what make the instrument stretch, what makes you go beyond the norm." -- Anonymous

An Idea to Write a Song About

You're at the theater. It's a movie you've been wanting to see for a long time. You have your large popcorn and a drink. Maybe even some nachos. Everything should be great. The only problem? You're alone...

Note Sequence for a Song

G-E-A-G-E

Power Words

Sailboat / Confetti / Scatter / Wheel / Fahrenheit

Cliches, Expressions, Slang and Idioms

- Easy as shooting fish in a barrel
- Happy as a hog in slop
- That's half the battle

Rolling Stone Magazine's Greatest Songs of all Time -- #4

WHAT'S GOING ON (Marvin Gaye) 1971 (Songwriters: Gaye/Benson/Cleveland)

A FEW LINES: "Mother, mother. / There's too many of you crying. / Brother, brother, brother. / There's far too many of you dying. / You know we've got to find a way. / To bring some lovin' here today."

DID YOU KNOW... Gaye was a talented football player and although he never played professionally, he was friends with Mel Farr and Lem Barney of the Detroit Lions. They used to greet each other with the expression "what's going on" which Gaye then used for the song title to this hit.

Songwriter's Toolkit

American Songwriter (Published 6 times a year)

This publication covers the full spectrum of American music, from the creative songwriting process to music business-related columns. Each issue contains interviews with the world's top songwriters and artists, as well as up-and-comers. *American Songwriter* strives to serve as "the unparalleled source of inspiration for passionate music fans and songwriters alike." ($19.95/year)

Songwriter Quote

*"I don't want you to play me a riff that's going to impress Joe Satriani; give me a riff that makes a kid want to go out and buy a guitar and learn to play." -- **Ozzy Osbourne***

SUNDAY

MONDAY

TUESDAY

WEDNESDAY

THURSDAY

FRIDAY

SATURDAY

Songwriting Exercise

Most songwriters create new songs accompanying themselves with an instrument as they progress through the songwriting process. This exercise is simple. Walk away from the keyboard or put down that guitar and begin writing your next song. Many times we get into a rut when we are playing an instrument and get stuck in the same key or use the same chord progressions. Writing without an instrument frees us of these boundaries.

Song Titles

- Tell Your Mother I'm Sorry
- Feeding Frenzy
- Slight Degrees Of Disagreement
- Double Dawg Dang
- Paper Promises

Chord Progression for a Song
C-D-F-G (I-II-IV-V)

Word Association Exercise

Close To _____   Under The _____

Nothing Like _____   Climbing The _____

When _____ Feels Like Nothing   Flash Of The _____

Songwriters Hall of Fame: Bruce Springsteen

Hall of Fame Induction: 1999. Springsteen is said to have brought rock and roll back to the working class. Forming several bands in his early years, he eventually went to the studio and released *Greetings from Asbury Park, N.J.* in 1973. But it was *Born In The U.S.A.* (1984) that put him over the top for good as it spawned seven hit singles and sold over 10 million copies. **Little known fact:** Interestingly enough, Springsteen has never had a #1 single on the Top 40 charts. *Dancing in the Dark* hit #2 in 1984, but was kept out of the top spot by *When Doves Cry* (Prince). **Recommended listening:** *Born to Run, Tunnel of Love* and *We Shall Overcome: The Seeger Sessions.*

---

*"Life is a great big canvas, and you should throw all the paint you can on it." -- **Danny Kaye***

Inspirational Quote

An Idea to Write a Song About

You are getting ready for your wedding. The day is nice and soft, soothing music plays in the background. You hear the Wedding March begin off in the distance. You take a deep breath. This should be easy. After all, you've already been married five times...

Note Sequence for a Song
B-B-B-G#-A-B

Power Words

Feather / Wand / Tattoo / Copper / Chessboard

Cliches, Expressions, Slang and Idioms
- It's not the end of the world
- The morals of an alley cat and scruples of a snake
- More than I bargained for

Rolling Stone Magazine's Greatest Songs of all Time -- #5

Respect (Aretha Franklin) 1967 (Songwriter: Otis Redding)
A FEW LINES: "What you want. / Baby, I got. / What you need. / Do you know I got it? / All I'm askin' is for a little respect when you come home."
DID YOU KNOW... This was Franklin's first song to hit the charts in England. It was written by Otis Redding who originally recorded it two years earlier. His version hit #35 on the U.S. charts.

Songwriter's Toolkit

How to Promote Your Music Successfully on the Internet
by David Nevue (Midnight Rain Productions)
Most musicians have no idea where to start when it comes to online promotion and distribution. Some get as far as putting up a web site, but stop there. Wouldn't it be great if people heard your music every single day? What if you could use your web site to sell dozens of CDs every month as well as digital downloads via *iTunes*, *Rhapsody*, *Yahoo* and other online retailers. That's the purpose of this book and it does it well. ($34.95; PDF $19.95)

Songwriter Quote

"I've always felt that blues, rock 'n' roll and country are just about a beat apart." -- **Waylon Jennings**

SUNDAY

MONDAY

TUESDAY

WEDNESDAY

THURSDAY

FRIDAY

SATURDAY

Songwriting Exercise

Try writing a song using only two chords. This is actually harder than it sounds especially if you want a melody that's not too monotonous. I've written two or three songs using only two chords. A buddy of mine wrote a song using only one chord, but you would never know it by listening to the song.

Song Titles

- Wear Your Wisdom Well
- Necromancer
- An Alexandrian Epic
- Crazy Cats
- I Got Off The Beaten Path (And Now I'm Lost)

Chord Progression for a Song
C-F-A♭-G (I-IV-VIb-V)

Word Association Exercises

Happy To _____

_____ Like A Lady

One Happy _____

Like The End Of _____

Like _____ In _____

_____ And Dog

Songwriters Hall of Fame: Billy Joel

Hall of Fame Induction: 1992. Billy Joel's early introduction to music came from the classical side as he still cites Beethoven, Chopin and Debussy among his favorite composers. Early on he was a member of several different rock bands including The Hassles which released two albums on the RCA label. *Cold Spring Harbor* was his first solo release, but was badly produced and a failure in the marketplace. However, his first album with Columbia Records, *Piano Man* was a different story. The album went Gold and the single made him a pop star. **Little known fact:** Joel's 12th album, *River of Dreams,* was released in 1993. The cover was painted by supermodel Christie Brinkley, his wife at the time. **Recommended listening:** *52nd Street, Glass Houses* and *An Innocent Man.*

"One man has enthusiasm for 30 minutes, another for 30 days, but it is the man who has it for 30 years who makes a success of his life."
-- Edward B. Butler

Inspirational Quote

An Idea to Write a Song About

Think about the movie you would rate as your "all-time" favorite film. Maybe even rent the DVD to refresh your memory. Then write a song about the movie, changing names and places as needed to make the song unique.

Note Sequence for a Song
A-E-A-E-F-A-E

Power Words

Mosaic / Flicker / Lighthouse / Pirate / Labyrinth

Cliches, Expressions, Slang and Idioms

- When your time is up
- If this is living, I'd rather be dead
- It takes a big dog to weigh a ton

Rolling Stone Magazine's Greatest Songs of all Time -- #6

GOOD VIBRATIONS (The Beach Boys) 1966 (Songwriters: Wilson/Love)
A FEW LINES: "I, I love the colorful clothes she wears. / And the way the sunlight plays upon her hair. / I hear the sound of a gentle word. / On the wind that lifts her perfume through the air."
DID YOU KNOW... This was the last #1 hit in the U.S. for The Beach Boys until *Kokomo* topped the charts 22 years later. It is the longest anyone has gone between #1 hits.

Songwriter's Toolkit

Rhyme Wizard (RhymeWizard.com)
Rhyming Software for Windows and Mac
With over 100,000 words and phrases, all cross-referenced to near rhymes, Rhyme Wizard is a great tool for any songwriter. The program was created by a songwriter and teacher whose goals were to create a rhyming dictionary with features most useful for writers. Simply type in a word or phrase and click. That's all there is to it. Its a great tool to add to your bag of tricks. It's not a crutch, but a faithful writing buddy that's there when you need it. ($29.95)

Songwriter Quote

"It seems to me that those songs that have been any good, I have nothing much to do with the writing of them. The words have just crawled down my sleeve and come out on the page." -- Joan Baez

SUNDAY

MONDAY

TUESDAY

WEDNESDAY

THURSDAY

FRIDAY

SATURDAY

Songwriting Exercise

Pick up today's newspaper and open it up to the obituaries. Quickly scan down the list until you find an obituary with a paragraph or two of information. Change the name of the person and then imagine what that person's life was like based on the information. This may sound a bit morbid, but think of it as a tribute of sorts. Maybe even write a song from the first person perspective and imagine what the final days of that person's life might have been like.

Song Titles

- The Mists Of Yesterday's Memories
- Do Computers Dream Of Pixelated Sheep?
- Sittin' On The Front Porch Swing
- Does Scotland Yard Have A Merry-Go-Round?
- Blink Once If You Love Me

Chord Progression for a Song
C-E-Am-F (I-III-vi-IV)

Word Association Exercises

Just One Of Those _____   _____ In A _____ Sky

Ode To _____   First, Last And _____

Easy As _____   Pretty As A _____

Songwriters Hall of Fame: Don McLean

Hall of Fame Induction: 2004. Ask any music aficionado what Don McLean is known for and the almost-unanimous answer will be *American Pie*, the single that hit #1 in 1971 and stayed on the charts for 17 weeks. He has also had 5 other Top 40 hits. In 1980 McLean had an international #1 hit with a cover version of Roy Orbison's *Crying*. McLean recently penned his autobiography, *Killing Us Softly: The Don McLean Story*. **Little known fact:** For several years, the Van Gogh Museum in Amsterdam played McLean's song *Vincent* daily. A copy of the sheet music is in a safe beneath the museum along with several Van Gogh items. **Recommended listening:** *American Pie, Chain Lightning* and *The Best of Don McLean*.

---

*"The line between failure and success is so fine that we scarcely know when we pass it - so fine that we often are on the line and do not know it." -- **Ralph Waldo Emerson***

Inspirational Quote

An Idea to Write a Song About

You've had a wonderful night at the carnival even though you went alone. You decided to end the evening with a good, old-fashioned ride on the ferris wheel. It's crowded, but a girl/guy in line doesn't mind if you share a seat. Amazingly enough, the ferris wheel breaks down and you're stranded at the top...

Note Sequence for a Song
C-A-C-E-C-A-G

Power Words
Frost / Pebble / Sawdust / Avalanche / Twinkle

Cliches, Expressions, Slang and Idioms
- A grain of salt
- The road to nowhere
- A thin line between love and hate

Rolling Stone Magazine's Greatest Songs of all Time -- #7
JOHNNY B. GOODE (Chuck Berry) 1958 (Songwriter: Berry)
A FEW LINES: "Deep down in Louisiana, close to New Orleans. / Way back up in the woods among the evergreens. / There stood a log cabin made of earth and wood. / Where lived a country boy named Johnny B. Goode."
DID YOU KNOW... One of the lines in the song, "That little country boy could play" was originally "That little colored boy can play." Berry knew that if he wanted radio play, he had to change the lyrics.

Songwriter's Toolkit
Melody in Songwriting: Tools and Techniques for Writing Hit Songs (Berklee Press Publications)
by Jack Perricone (ISBN: 063400638X)
This comprehensive guide unlocks the secrets of hit songs, examines them and then reveals why they succeeded. It also teaches you how to write memorable melodies and discover the dynamic relationships between melody, harmony, rhythm and rhyme. ($24.95)

Songwriter Quote

"But I've got to think of myself as the luckiest guy. Robert Johnson only had one album's worth of work as his legacy. That's all that life allowed him." -- David Bowie

SUNDAY

MONDAY

TUESDAY

WEDNESDAY

THURSDAY

FRIDAY

SATURDAY

Songwriting Exercise

Walk out your front door and wait for the next vehicle to drive by. Car, truck or van. It doesn't really matter. Now try to imagine the person that owns that car. Are they rich? Are they a struggling single mom barely able to put dinner on the table? Is it a delivery guy singing songs behind the wheel who can't wait to get home to his family? Put them in a special situation or simply write a song about how they are feeling or what obstacles they might be facing that day.

Song Titles

- Melt Like Ice
- Corduroy
- Do They Have Email In Heaven?
- If Wishes Were Fishes
- It Could Have Turned Out Better (You're Still Breathing)

Chord Progression for a Song
Am-C-Dm-G (i-III-iv-VII)

Word Association Exercises

_____ Companion

In The Heat Of _____

Seeds Of _____

_____ Hands

_____ Morning

Calling _____

Songwriters Hall of Fame: Neil Diamond

Hall of Fame Induction: 1984. Neil Diamond began his recording career in 1966 when *Cherry Cherry* hit the charts. Ironically, his first #1 single as a songwriter came with the 1967 Monkees release, *I'm A Believer* and his first personal chart topper didn't come until 1970 when *Cracklin' Rosey* rose to the #1 position. In 1999, he was named one of the top five concert artists of the decade by Amusement Business Magazine. **Little known fact:** Diamond was awarded a fencing scholarship to New York University. **Recommended listening:** *The Essential Neil Diamond, Beautiful Noise* and *You Don't Bring Me Flowers*.

"To accomplish great things, we must not only act, but also dream; not only plan, but also believe." -- Anatole France

Inspirational Quote

An Idea to Write a Song About
Remember when you were a child? The world was innocent. You didn't think about money or your health or the crime rate. Life was just, well, innocent. Write a song about the difference between life as a child and life as an adult.

Note Sequence for a Song
D-D-C-C-F-F-E

Power Words
Autumn / Pyramid / Shuffle / Rattlesnake / Sandstone

Cliches, Expressions, Slang and Idioms
- No fool like an old fool
- Running in circles
- Squeaky wheel

Rolling Stone Magazine's Greatest Songs of all Time -- #8
HEY JUDE (The Beatles) 1968 (Songwriters: Lennon/McCartney)
A FEW LINES: "Hey Jude, don't make it bad. / Take a sad song and make it better. / Remember to let her into your heart. / Then you can start to make it better."
DID YOU KNOW... This song begins with one instrument (piano) and ends with 50. The fadeout at the end of the song takes 4 minutes and the chorus is repeated 19 times.

Songwriter's Toolkit
OnlineRock Short Run CDs (OnlineRock.com) (650) 649-2304.
Most CD reproduction houses start their packages at 1,000 CDs or more. But if you have an EP or just want to send around a demo, why would you want to get that many CDs printed at once? It's expensive and many CDs could go to waste. *OnlineRock* can produce short run CDRs from your CD master with full color printing and order as few as 10 CDs at a time. It's perfect for songwriters and bands who want to market themselves in a professional manner whether it's for demos, radio station promos or sales.

"Music is a higher revelation than all wisdom and philosophy. Music is the electrical soil in which the spirit lives, thinks and invents." **-- Ludwig van Beethoven**

SUNDAY

MONDAY

TUESDAY

WEDNESDAY

THURSDAY

FRIDAY

SATURDAY

Songwriting Exercise

Take out pen and pencil and write a letter to someone you know. Choose some-one you'd love to write to and say something that you'd never say in real life. Maybe it's a love letter or maybe it's something you've always wanted to tell them, but were afraid to. Maybe it's something you always wanted to tell your mother or father. Or your boss. Or your ex-girlfriend or boyfriend. After you write the letter, take the ideas you've expressed and write a song about it. (And then maybe you want to tear up the letter!)

Song Titles

- Rabbit On The Run
- You Make Me Glad To Be Me
- When The Shadows Touch You
- Like Heaven On Wheels
- Just An Old Temperamental Fool

Chord Progression for a Song
C-B♭-A♭-Gm (I-VII♭-VI♭-v)

Word Association Exercises

Broken _____   Laughter Like _____

In The Middle Of A _____   _____ Sunglasses

Gray As _____   _____ And Stones

Songwriters Hall of Fame: John Fogerty

Hall of Fame Induction: 1988. As a member of Creedence Clearwater Revival, Fogerty penned nine Top Ten singles between 1969 and 1972. The band also scored eight gold albums during that period. Fogerty also had six Top 40 hits as a solo artist with his *Centerfield* album hitting #1 on the charts. Creedence was inducted into the Rock and Roll Hall of Fame in 1993. **Little known fact:** Fogerty released an album of Creedence covers in 1973 on which he played all the instruments under the name the Blue Ridge Rangers. **Recommended listening:** *Willie and the Poor Boys, Green River* and *Centerfield.*

"No dreamer is ever too small; no dream is ever too big." --
Anonymous

Inspirational Quote

An Idea to Write a Song About

Think back about a time you got together with your family. Maybe it was a family reunion or a holiday get-together. Try and remember who was there and what made the day memorable. Crazy cousin Al? Great Grandmother Minerva? The turkey that was cooked too long? There are probably several song ideas in just that one day.

Note Sequence for a Song
F-F-B♭-B♭-A-A-C

Power Words
Jewel / Bronze / Flight / Thorn / Canticle

Cliches, Expressions, Slang and Idioms
- Left in the lurch
- Until the cows come home
- The sun don't shine on the same dog's behind everyday

Rolling Stone Magazine's Greatest Songs of all Time -- #9
SMELLS LIKE TEEN SPIRIT (Nirvana) 1991
(Songwriter: Kurt Cobain)
A FEW LINES: "With the lights out, it's less dangerous. / Here we are now, entertain us. / I feel stupid and contagious. / Here we are now, entertain us."
DID YOU KNOW... Kurt Cobain didn't know that *Teen Spirit* was a brand of deodorant marketed to young girls when he wrote this song. Sales of the product greatly increased when the song became a hit.

Songwriter's Toolkit
Webster's New World Thesaurus (Webster's New World)
by Charlton Laird (ISBN: 0743470729)
This thesaurus is organized alphabetically with no confusing number systems. Only common words are used in the main entry list so you're not wading through a list of esoteric words that you would not think of looking for. It is filled with synonyms, antonyms and phrases other word finding reference books sometime overlook so you're never at a loss for words. ($21.99)

Songwriter Quote

"My daughter thought I sang with the Everly Brothers ... I said, 'no I was one of the Righteous Brothers' and she said 'didn't they invent the airplane?'" -- **Bill Medley**

SUNDAY

MONDAY

TUESDAY

WEDNESDAY

THURSDAY

FRIDAY

SATURDAY

Songwriting Exercise

Try writing a song using variations of every note in the scale. In other words, A, B, C, D, E F and G. You can use variations of the chords to make it easier. For example you can use minor chords, 7th chords, augmented chords, etc. And to make it a bit easier, you can even use flats and sharps. This is actually not as hard as it sounds. I've done this once (although it was completely accidental), so I know it can be done without sounding forced or strange.

Song Titles

- Lips Like Licorice
- Painted Ponies
- Pocket Change
- I Thought I Saw My Shadow Dancing
- The Strike Of The Snake, The Sting Of The Bee

Chord Progression for a Song
C-Am-F-C (I-vi-IV-I)

Word Association Exercise

Angels And _____

_____ And Soda Pop

That _____ Tingle

Love Like _____

_____ Airplanes

The Colors Of _____

Songwriters Hall of Fame: Carole King

Hall of Fame Induction: 1987. King's success as a songwriter was cemented in 1960 when The Shirelle's *Will You Still Love Me Tomorrow?* (which she co-wrote with future husband and songwriting partner Gerry Goffin) hit #1 on the charts. But it was not until 11 years later that she hit stride as a recording artist in her own right with the release of *Tapestry* which stayed on the charts for six years and garnered her four Grammy awards. **Little known fact:** King attended Queens College with Goffin, Paul Simon and Neil Sedaka. Sedaka had a hit with *Oh Carol* which was about King. **Recommended listening:** *Tapestry, Her Greatest Hits: Songs of Long Ago* and *Rhymes and Reasons*.

---

*"Poets need not go to Niagara to write about the force of falling water". -- **Robert Frost***

Inspirational Quote

An Idea to Write a Song About

"She loves me. She loves me not." We've all probably done this while picking petals off a flower. And, of course, there are more than a few songs like this. So take the idea and change it up. Maybe "she loves me" ends up not being the case. Maybe you end up being allergic to the flower.

Note Sequence for a Song
G-C-F-E-D-E-C

Power Words
Beach / Chocolate / Whisper / Swamp / Orient

Cliches, Expressions, Slang and Idioms
• The sun in your eyes made some of the lies worth believing
• As cute as a button
• All dressed up and nowhere to go

Rolling Stone Magazine's Greatest Songs of all Time -- #10
WHAT'D I SAY (Ray Charles) 1959 (Songwriter: Charles)
A FEW LINES: "Hey mama, don't you treat me wrong. / Come and love your daddy all night long. / All right now, hey hey, all right."
DID YOU KNOW... Charles literally wrote this in front of an audience. He was told after his last number he still had 12 minutes to fill. He told his band to follow his lead and his backing singers to simply repeat whatever he said.

Songwriter's Toolkit
Performing Songwriter (Published 8 times a year)
Performing Songwriter has always been one of my favorite magazines. (Maybe it's because I met editor Lydia Hutchinson once at the Rocky Mountain Folks Festival in Lyons, Colorado and found her very knowledgeable about the singer/songwriter scene and very personable at the same time.) The publications covers everything from finding inspiration to the tools necessary for songwriters to get their music on stage, into the studio and into the hands of listeners. ($4.95/single issue or $25.95/year)

Songwriter Quote

"Great songwriters don't always choose to hang in this lifestyle and this profession and try to make a go of it. They find other jobs, they have families and they continue to write, but you're never going to hear their songs." -- Shawn Colvin

SUNDAY

MONDAY

TUESDAY

WEDNESDAY

THURSDAY

FRIDAY

SATURDAY

Songwriting Exercise

Tell the complete story of your life in three or four minutes. The object is to create a collage of music that highlights the most memorable moments of your life whether they are good, bad or indifferent. (Think *One Week* by The Barenaked Ladies or *We Didn't Start the Fire* by Billy Joel.)

Song Titles

- Stop Me If You've Heard This
- Waking Up In Wonderland
- Butterflies And Alibis
- Walls Without Windows
- Shooting Stars, Old Guitars And Milky Way Candy Bars

Chord Progression for a Song
C-Em-F-Em (I-iii-IV-iii)

Word Association Exercises

Quiet As A _____

You're Still _____

Waiting For _____

_____ Rainbow

Miles And Miles From _____

I Can Hear The _____

Songwriters Hall of Fame: Jeff Barry/Ellie Greenwich

Hall of Fame Induction: 1991. Jeff Barry and Ellie Greenwich joined forces in the early 1960s as husband and wife and as songwriting partners. They became one of the most prolific and successful Brill Building songwriting teams in history. If you don't recognize the names, think about titles like *Leader of the Pack, Then He Kissed Me, River Deep, Mountain High* and *Chapel of Love*. **Little known fact:** Don Kirshner asked Barry to produce some tracks for a new group. He had with him a Neil Diamond tune called *I'm A Believer* which the Monkees took to #1 on the charts where it remained for 7 weeks. **Recommended listening:** Although Barry and Greenwich wrote hundreds of successful songs, they never became successful performers in their own right.

---

*"Obstacles are those frightful things you see when you take your eyes off your goals." -- **Anonymous***

Inspirational Quote

An Idea to Write a Song About

Pretend you're a kid who's dreaming of being a sports star. The chorus could be generic about the "dream" while each verse could focus on a different sporting event. For example, one verse could be about catching the game-winning pass in the Super Bowl and another about winning a NASCAR race.

Note Sequence for a Song
F-F-A-A-G-G-B♭

Power Words
Danger / Willow / Bridge / Schooner / Flint

Cliches, Expressions, Slang and Idioms
- Doing the slow burn
- A snowball's chance in hell
- Holding down the fort

Rolling Stone Magazine's Greatest Songs of all Time -- #11
MY GENERATION (The Who) 1965 (Songwriter: Pete Townshend)
A FEW LINES: "Why don't you all f-fade away. / And don't try to dig what we all s-s-say. / I'm not trying to cause a big s-s-sensation. / I'm just talkin' 'bout my g-g-g-generation."
DID YOU KNOW... During a 1967 television performance, Keith Moon set his drums to explode not knowing the tech crew had already done it. The resulting explosion burned Townshend's hair and permanently damaged his hearing.

Songwriter's Toolkit
Nashville Songwriter's Association International (nashvillesongwriters.com)
Established in 1967, the Nashville Songwriters Association International (NSAI) is the world's largest not-for-profit trade organization dedicated to serving songwriters of all genres of music. With national and regional chapters, it is a great source of information including regional workshops and discounts on other stuff that belong in your songwriter's toolkit. Membership rate is $150.00 a year. 1-800-321-6008

Songwriter Quote

"The only Maybelline I knew was the name of a cow".
-- Chuck Berry

SUNDAY

MONDAY

TUESDAY

WEDNESDAY

THURSDAY

FRIDAY

SATURDAY

Songwriting Exercise

There have been lots of hit tunes written about America and patriotism. Unfortunately, many of these tunes were inspired by and written during times of war. Even America's national anthem was written while Francis Scott Key observed the assault on Fort McHenry by the British in 1814. Patriotic songs always seem to inspire us in one form or another. *Born in the U.S.A.* by Bruce Springsteen, *God Bless the U.S.A.* by Lee Greenwood or Woody Guthrie's *This Land Is Your Land*. Now it's your turn to write a song about your homeland.

Song Titles

- All Alone In Heaven
- Crocodiles Don't Smile, They Grin
- Wooden Shoes
- I Got The Merry-Go-Round Blues
- Give Me Some Crackers, I'm Thirsty

Chord Progression for a Song
Am-Dm-E (i-iv-V)

Word Association Exercises

Back In _____ Again

A Bottle Full Of _____

Ain't No Place Like _____

Never Enough _____

Life After _____

A _____ New Day

Songwriters Hall of Fame: Randy Newman

Hall of Fame Induction: 2002. Even though most people familiar with Randy Newman know him for his career as a performer and songwriter, it is his numerous tunes composed for movies that have earned him a widespread reputation. Many of his songs are very political in nature although the messages are hidden in well-crafted song and verse. He has won many awards including an Emmy, an Oscar and three Grammys. **Little known fact:** Newman was briefly a member of The Tikis who later became Harpers Bizarre, best known for their cover version of Paul Simon's *Feelin' Groovy*. **Recommended listening:** *Sail Away, Little Criminals* and *Land of Dreams*.

"Remember when you see a man at the top of a mountain, he didn't fall there." -- Anonymous

Inspirational Quote

An Idea to Write a Song About
You've just bought your dream house. It's everything you thought it would be. But, of course, things change once you buy it and move in. Now the paint is peeling, the water faucets are leaking and the furnace doesn't work!

Note Sequence for a Song
C-B♭-A-G-A-B♭-A

Power Words
Hacienda / Lightning / Mask / Crown / Sigh

Cliches, Expressions, Slang and Idioms
- Play with the hand you're dealt
- If a frog had wings
- Reading the riot act

Rolling Stone Magazine's Greatest Songs of all Time -- #12
A CHANGE IS GONNA COME (Sam Cooke) 1965 (Songwriter: Cooke)
A FEW LINES: "I was born by the river in a little tent. / And just like the river, I've been running ever since. / It's been a long time coming. / But I know a change is gonna come."
DID YOU KNOW... Cooke wrote this after hearing Bob Dylan's *Blowin' In The Wind*. He couldn't believe the song wasn't written by a black man. He felt compelled to write something from a similar perspective. Ironically, it wasn't released until after his death.

Songwriter's Toolkit
Songwriters on Songwriting (Da Capo Press)
by Paul Zollo (ISBN: 0306812657)
This book is a collection of interviews in which luminaries of popular songwriting (including Bob Dylan, Carole King, Paul Simon, Randy Newman and Madonna) discuss the ins and outs of the songwriting process and the origins of their classics. It includes practitioners from different genres of popular music in original interviews conducted by *SongTalk* magazine. ($22.95)

Songwriter Quote

"I think its so cool that you can pick up the guitar and create something that didn't exist 5 minutes ago. You can write something that no one has ever heard before. You have music at your fingertips." -
- Michelle Branch

SUNDAY

MONDAY

TUESDAY

WEDNESDAY

THURSDAY

FRIDAY

SATURDAY

Songwriting Exercise

This is an exercise that incorporates speed into your songwriting. Although speed isn't really important when you are writing a song, it is important not to get bogged down in too much tweaking as you go. So get out your stop watch and write a complete song in ten minutes. It's important that you time yourself and that you finish within the allotted time no matter what you end up with. This exercise will strengthen your ability to write without editing as you go. It's important to get your thoughts on to paper at this point without too many detours along the way.

Song Titles

- Darkness Never Dances
- Do The Undead Snore When They Sleep?
- Prophets In Tuxedos
- Sandstorm
- Falling Down In Flowered Fields

Chord Progression for a Song
    C-Em-F-G (I-iii-IV-V)

Word Association Exercises

Passion And _____

_____ And Chocolate

Going For The _____

Most Of The Time I Just _____

Money And _____

As Old As _____

Songwriters Hall of Fame: Otis Redding

Hall of Fame Induction: 1994. Redding made his first records in 1960 with his group, Otis and the Shooters. Two years later he hit the charts with *These Arms* and built his fan base with an electrifying touring show. He had a series of successful songs from that time on both as an artist and as a songwriter. **Little known fact:** *Dock of the Bay,* Redding's signature song, was released after his death and became the first posthumous #1 hit on the Billboard charts. **Recommended listening:** *Dock of the Bay, Otis Blue: Otis Redding Sings Love Songs* and *In Person at the Whiskey a Go Go.*

---

*"You pile up enough tomorrows, and you'll find you've collected a lot of empty yesterdays." -- **Professor Harold Hill** (The Music Man)*

Inspirational Quote

An Idea to Write a Song About

You're a young boy in grade school who gets picked on every day by the school bully. One day you decide that it's time to stand up to him. Maybe you lose, maybe you win, but at least you took a stand against him.

Note Sequence for a Song
G-C-B-C-B-C-G

Power Words
Ten / Slumber / Sinister / Neon / Spider

Cliches, Expressions, Slang and Idioms
- Ugly to the bone
- With the wind at your back
- Like a freight train off the track

Rolling Stone Magazine's Greatest Songs of all Time -- #13
YESTERDAY (The Beatles) 1965 (Songwriters: Lennon/McCartney)
A FEW LINES: "Yesterday. / All my troubles seemed so far away. / Now it feels as though they're here to stay. / Oh I believe in yesterday."
DID YOU KNOW... The working title to this hit was *Scrambled Eggs*. It was the first Beatles' tune to feature only one band member (Paul McCartney) and was actually vetoed by the other three members of the group for release in the U.K. as a single for that reason. (It was finally released there in 1976.)

Songwriter's Toolkit
Cakewalk Home Studio (Cakewalk)
Software for Windows 98 / 2000 / XP / Me / NT
This solid software program comes with comprehensive features that turns your computer into a multitrack recording studio, giving you everything you need to take your music from inspiration to CD. If you have a PC and you are looking for an inexpensive entry-level sequencer that will record both audio and midi, take a look at this one. Although not as easy to use as *GarageBand* (Mac), this is probably the best entry-level alternative for PC users. ($149.99)

Songwriter Quote

"I've written many extra verses to songs that I learned to sing - an extra verse about a friend, or just add some verse - and that led to writing my own songs." -- Jackson Browne

SUNDAY

MONDAY

TUESDAY

WEDNESDAY

THURSDAY

FRIDAY

SATURDAY

Songwriting Exercise

Take the "ten-minute" song you wrote in the previous exercise. Now sharpen your pencil and begin the editing process. There are very few situations where a song is finished the first time through. Even songwriters who claim they finished a song in ten minutes probably end up at some point changing a few words now and then. I have songs that I wrote thirty years ago that get a word changed here and there occasionally. So take that song and begin editing. Make the lyrics stronger. Make the rhymes better. Add a bridge if it needs it. But most of all, just try to improve it until it feels finished. At least for the moment...

Song Titles

- Close Your Eyes And Dance With Me
- She Should Have Been Happy
- If You Think You're Free, You're Crazy As Me
- Mantra
- And The Pages Yellow With Age

Chord Progression for a Song
C-E-F-Fm (I-III-IV-iv)

Word Association Exercises

Flowers Of _____   Hanging By A _____

Cold, Cold _____   In The Darkness Of _____

Smiles That Remind Me Of _____   Faster Than _____

Songwriters Hall of Fame: Dianne Warren

Hall of Fame Induction: 2001. Want a short list of Warren's songs recorded by others? It's nothing short of amazing. How about Aretha Franklin, Celine Dion, Trisha Yearwood, Cher, Aerosmith and that barely nicks the surface. She was the first songwriter in the Billboard history to have seven hits, all by different artists, on the singles chart at the same time. **Little known fact:** Warren's songs have been included in more than 80 movies. **Recommended listening:** *Because You Loved Me: Songs of Diane Warren* by Johnny Mathis and *Diane Warren Presents: Love Songs*.

"When you reach for the stars, you may not get one, but you won't come up with a handful of mud, either". -- Anonymous

Inspirational Quote

An Idea to Write a Song About

You're sauntering along downtown minding your own business when you see a girl/guy walking out of a store. And you think to yourself "I never thought I believed in love at first sight, but now..."

Note Sequence for a Song
G-B-A-C-E-D-C-D-C-B

Power Words
Gloom / Dusk / Dizzy / Burgundy / Serpent

Cliches, Expressions, Slang and Idioms
• A half hour in heaven
• A road paved with good intentions
• Chasing rainbows

Rolling Stone Magazine's Greatest Songs of all Time -- #14
BLOWIN' IN THE WIND (Bob Dylan) 1963 (Songwriter: Dylan)
A FEW LINES: "How many roads must a man walk down. / Before you call him a man? / And how many seas must a white dove sail. / Before she sleeps in the sand? / And how many times must the cannon balls fly. / Before they're forever banned? / The answer, my friend, is blowin' in the wind."
DID YOU KNOW... Dylan was an obscure folk singer when he wrote this, but became a rising star when it became an international hit for Peter, Paul and Mary. He gained national recognition when he performed this with the trio at the 1963 Newport Folk Festival.

Songwriter's Toolkit
Dirty Linen (Published 6 times a year)
Dirty Linen has been around as long as I remember and is still the great publication it has always been. Bi-monthly issues contain interviews, record reviews, personality sketches and news of folk, folk-rock and traditional music concerts. Coverage is international in scope although most interest is devoted to American musicians. ($4.99/single issue or $22/year)

Songwriter Quote

"You know, a song is like a kid. You bring it up. And sometimes something you thought was going to be fantastic, by the time it's finished, is a bit of a disappointment." -- Phil Collins

SUNDAY

MONDAY

TUESDAY

WEDNESDAY

THURSDAY

FRIDAY

SATURDAY

Songwriting Exercise

Take a cliche or well-known phrase and add a few words to make that cliche something new and different. For example, take the cliche (and Rolling Stones' song) *Time Is On My Side*. Now change it to something different or unexpected. How about "Time Is On My Side, But It Seems I Was Just Lying On My Alarm Clock" or "Time Is On My Side, But There's Lightning In The Sky." Anyway, you get the idea.

Song Titles

- Silly Things You Say When You're Asleep
- My Heart Stops Everytime I See You (But I Never Say Hello)
- One Step Beyond The Cliff
- Urban Lifestyle
- Gravity Just Pulls Us Down

Chord Progression for a Song
C-F-E-G (I-IV-III-V)

Word Association Exercises

_____ Of The Soul

Poetry And _____

Dressed Up And _____

Strong _____

Too _____ To _____

_____ And A Blue Moon

Songwriters Hall of Fame: Roy Orbison

Hall of Fame Induction: 1989. Roy Orbison was one of the early pioneers of rock and roll with a career that covered more than four decades. Known for hits such as *Pretty Woman, Only the Lonely* and *Crying*, he had 23 Top 40 hits. Ironically, his first successful song was one called *Ooby Dooby* which he didn't even write although he is usually given a songwriting credit for the number. **Little known fact:** Beginning in August of 1963 and continuing for 68 straight weeks, Orbison was the only American performer to have #1 singles on the British charts. **Recommended listening:** *Crying, Mystery Girl* and *The Complete Sun Sessions*.

"*After all is said and done, there is usually more said than done.*" - *- Anonymous*

Inspirational Quote

An Idea to Write a Song About
You're hitchhiking down a deserted stretch of road. It's been hours since a vehicle passed by and they must have been doing at least 70. You're hungry and you're cold. In fact, snowflakes are beginning to fall and dusk isn't far away...

Note Sequence for a Song
D-G-D-D-A-G-A-G-F-E-D-C-D

Power Words
Gothic / Catacomb / Carriage / Moonstone / Cottage

Cliches, Expressions, Slang and Idioms
• The point of no return
• Call in the dogs and let's go home
• Like a three ring circus

Rolling Stone Magazine's Greatest Songs of all Time -- #15
LONDON CALLING (The Clash) 1979 (Songwriters: Jones/Stummer)
A FEW LINES: "The ice age is coming, the sun's zooming in. / Meltdown expected, the wheat is growing thin. / Engines stop running, but I have no fear. / 'Cause London is drowning and I live by the river."
DID YOU KNOW... Even though this was named by Rolling Stone magazine as the 15th greatest song of all time, it was never released as a single in the U.S. *Train in Vain* was released instead and reached #23 on the U.S. charts.

Songwriter's Toolkit
The Craft and Business of Songwriting (Writer's Digest Books)
by John Braheny (ISBN: 1582970858)
John Braheny teaches the craft of songwriting while going behind the scenes of the music business to reveal insider secrets that will make your work stand out. Dozens of exercises, examples and anecdotes will you show you how to develop a songwriter's consciousness, overcome barriers in the creative process, write in all musical styles as well as skillfully manage the business of demos and contracts. ($22.99)

*"I'm a communicator, I like to communicate and if a million people buy it then we've touched a million people, if only 10 people buy it, then we've only touched 10, and that's important, because I'm satisfied with only 10. But, I love a million." -- **Graham Nash***

SUNDAY

MONDAY

TUESDAY

WEDNESDAY

THURSDAY

FRIDAY

SATURDAY

Songwriting Exercise

We all tend to write songs from a first person perspective. Try writing a song from second person or third person perspective. If writing in 2nd person, stay away from the words "I" and "me" even if it is someone close to you. In third person, think of someone famous and write a song about them, telling their story in your song. Think Bob Dylan's *Hurricane*, *Rock On* by David Essex. or *Man On The Moon* by R.E.M.

Song Titles

- Nancy Drew Didn't Have A Clue
- Old Dusty Boxes In The Back Of The Attic
- Her, She's Like Chocolate
- I Guess Destiny Doesn't Like Me Very Much
- Clowns In The Closet

Chord Progression for a Song
C-G-A♭-B♭ (I-V-VI♭-VII♭)

Word Association Exercises

Crooked As _____   _____ Of Time

_____ And Love   Stranger Than _____

A Dollar And A _____   Sorrow And _____

Songwriters Hall of Fame: Lionel Richie

Hall of Fame Induction: 1994. It's hard to say whether Richie is better known for his years as a member of The Commodores or as a solo artist. The Commodores had 17 songs hit the Top 40 charts between 1974 and 1985 while Ritchie himself had 16 songs on the charts between 1981 and 1996. He has also written hits for others including *Lady* for Kenny Rogers which spent six weeks at #1 in 1980. **Little known fact:** Richie's career in music started by accident when five Tuskegee University classmates asked him to join a band they were forming called The Mystics. The band later changed their name to The Commodores. **Recommended listening:** *Can't Slow Down, Dancing on the Ceiling* and *Coming Home*.

---

*"Every artist was first an amateur." -- **Ralph Waldo Emerson***

An Idea to Write a Song About

You're stranded on an island in the Pacific. The weather's great, the water's fantastic, the beach is phenomenal and you have plenty to eat. You are stranded there with a good looking girl/guy who seems to like you. There is a raft on the beach, but it is only large enough for one. What do you do?

Note Sequence for a Song
B-B-B-B-B-G-A

Power Words
Silence / Jungle / Demon / Leather / Straw

Cliches, Expressions, Slang and Idioms
- Does my heart good
- Bite the bullet
- Misery loves company

Rolling Stone Magazine's Greatest Songs of all Time -- #16
I WANT TO HOLD YOUR HAND (The Beatles) 1963
(Songwriters: Lennon/McCartney)
A FEW LINES: "Oh yeah, I´ll tell you something. / I think you'll understand. / When I say that something. / I wanna hold your hand. / I wanna hold your hand. / I wanna hold your hand."
DID YOU KNOW... This was the first Beatles' song to be recorded using 4-track equipment. Earlier Beatles' songs were mono recordings. This was also The Beatles' first number one song on the Billboard Hot 100 chart in the U.S.

Songwriter's Toolkit
Fostex Model X-12 Multi-Track Recorder
The X-12 has become one of the lowest-ever priced multi-track recorders. Its features includes simple one-track recording, quick and easy record track select button, 5-segment LED input level meter, individual playback level and pan control, stereo line out and headphone out with level control for stereo mastering or monitoring and much more. A solid investment. ($199.00)

Songwriter Quote

"All the good music has already been written by people with wigs and stuff." -- Frank Zappa

SUNDAY

MONDAY

TUESDAY

WEDNESDAY

THURSDAY

FRIDAY

SATURDAY

Songwriting Exercise

I've used the following songwriting "tool" on more than one occasion and usually to a pretty good success ratio. Write a song from the viewpoint of a child. Think back on your childhood and write something that reflects how you felt about it at the time. This has probably been done more often in country music than other genres, but don't let that stop you. Two examples of my own songs are *Monsters In The Dark* written from the perspective of a young boy afraid to go to sleep at night and *American Flyer* about the thrills of bike riding back in the good old days.

Song Titles

- She Sadly Saves Her Smiles For Some Far Off Rainy Day
- Tornadoes In December
- Gyroscope
- A Stranger Said She Loved Me, Do You Know Her?
- Lancelot Never Danced A Lot

Chord Progression for a Song
Am-C-F-G (i-III-VI-VII)

Word Association Exercises

Towers Of _____

Boxes Full Of _____

Cold As _____

Feeling Like A _____

Can't Seem To _____ You

_____ Of The Mind

Songwriters Hall of Fame: Carole Bayer Sager

Hall of Fame Induction: 1987. Although Carole Bayer Sager had a somewhat successful career as a performer, she is far better known as a songwriter. Whether she was writing solo or with the likes of Marvin Hamlisch, Burt Bacharach or David Foster, she seemed to have that "golden touch", beginning in 1966 with *Groovy Kind of Love* for The Mindbenders. **Little known fact:** Sager has the unique distinction of being married to both Hamlisch and Bacharach. **Recommended listening:** *Carole Bayer Sager, Sometimes Late at Night* and *Too.*

"The first thing an unpublished author should remember is that no one asked him to write in the first place. With this firmly in mind, he has no right to become discouraged just because other people are being published." -- John Farrar

Inspirational Quote

An Idea to Write a Song About

You just purchased a bag of Fritos and a Slurpee at your favorite convenience store. You also bought a lottery ticket just for the heck of it. You get to your car and begin scratching off the numbers. The first number matches your pick, then the second, then the third until you reach the final number. You take a deep breath and begin to scratch the ticket to reveal...

Note Sequence for a Song
A-C#-B-D-A-F-F-E-A

Power Words
Prance / Silk / Freeze / Igloo / Wink

Cliches, Expressions, Slang and Idioms
- Cheese and whine
- Back to square one
- Stealing victory

Rolling Stone Magazine's Greatest Songs of all Time -- #17
PURPLE HAZE (Jimi Hendrix) 1967 (Songwriter: Hendrix)
A FEW LINES: "Purple haze all in my brain. / Lately things just don't seem the same. / Acting funny but I don't know why. / 'Scuse me while I kiss the sky."
DID YOU KNOW... Although many people thought this song was a reference to drugs, Hendrix stated that it was simply inspired by a dream he had in which he was surrounded by a "purple haze."

Songwriter's Toolkit
The Indie Bible
by David Wimble (ISBN: 0968621457)
The book lists thousands of places where you can get your music reviewed and songs played. The contacts listed are reviewers and radio personalities from around the world that will listen to your music, and if they like it, present it to readers and listeners. It includes hundreds of publications that review CDs and radio stations that will might play your songs and much more. ($29.95)

Songwriter Quote

"I've always thought of music as something which gives the words their flight and their wings and the music often comes first, although sometimes I'll have a concept, a title idea, a lyric idea that I want to write and the lyric will come first." -- Neil Diamond

SUNDAY

MONDAY

TUESDAY

WEDNESDAY

THURSDAY

FRIDAY

SATURDAY

Songwriting Exercise

Here's an exercise to make your songs stronger. Take a song you've already finished. Now go through the song and take a look at your verbs, adjectives, adverbs and nouns. Can you change a word to make the lyrics stronger? Can you change the verb "talk" to "shout" or "moan"? Can you change the noun "black" to "indigo"? Don't be afraid to use a thesaurus or word finder. The strength of your words will separate your lyrics from thousands of other songs.

Song Titles
- I Thought I Saw An Angel
- The Party Died When She Went Home
- Texas Ace
- Takin' Out The Trash
- Livin' On Cruise Control

Chord Progression for a Song
C-B♭-Am-G (I-VII♭-vi-V)

Word Association Exercises

Each And Every _____

In The Quiet Of _____

_____ Like Time

Why Did You _____

Funny As A _____

Empty _____

Songwriters Hall of Fame: Harlan Howard

Hall of Fame Induction: 1997. Unfortunately for much for the world, the name Harlan Howard "rings no bells." But if you live in Nashville or are a country music fan, you probably recognize the name in an instant. Remember Patsy Cline's hit *I Fall to Pieces?* Or how about *Tiger By The Tail* from Buck Owens or *Heartaches By The Numbers* which was a hit for both Ray Price and Guy Mitchell? They were all written or co-written by Harlan Howard. **Little known fact:** Howard was named Billboard's Songwriter of the Year two years straight. **Recommended listening:** *Harlan Howard: All Time Favorite Country Songwriter, Buck Owens Sings Harlan Howard* and *Waylon Jennings Sings Ol' Harlan.*

---

*"The toughest thing about success is that you've got to keep on being a success. Talent is only a starting point in business. You've got to keep working that talent." -- **Irving Berlin***

Inspirational Quote

An Idea to Write a Song About

You're at the airport. You've been away two long weeks on a business trip. You can't wait to get home to your significant other whom you've missed so much. With ticket in hand you jog to the departure gate. Then you hear the announcement that your flight has been delayed indefinitely...

Note Sequence for a Song
G-G#-G-G#-B-E-G-F#

Power Words
Crimson / Gospel / Scratch / Cinnamon / Sagebrush

Cliches, Expressions, Slang and Idioms
- Slow boat to china
- Counting the days
- Last straw

Rolling Stone Magazine's Greatest Songs of all Time -- #18
MAYBELLINE (Chuck Berry) 1955 (Songwriter: Berry)
A FEW LINES: "Maybellene, why can't you be true? / Oh Maybellene, why can't you be true? / You've started back doing the things you used to do."
DID YOU KNOW... Disc jockey Alan Freed gained a songwriting credit for *Maybelline* for playing it on the radio. Deals such as this eventually led to the famous "payola" scandals after which playing songs on the radio for pay was prohibited.

Songwriter's Toolkit
Studio Aid
Studio Aid is an online recording studio offering custom guitar tracks, drum tracks and bass backing tracks at affordable rates. They offer professional quality musicianship at a fraction of the price of a walk-in studio. Completed session work is provided via download in the form of digital audio files or on CD. At only $34 per session track, there might not be a better way to make your demos sound better. **(www.studio-aid.com)**

*"If you can't play it on an acoustic guitar or a grand piano then it's not a song." -- **Christopher Cross***

SUNDAY

MONDAY

TUESDAY

WEDNESDAY

THURSDAY

FRIDAY

SATURDAY

Songwriting Exercise

Write a happy song. Now this is actually a much harder exercise than it sounds. And to make it even a little more difficult, do not make it a love song. We're not looking for a repeat of *Don't Worry, Be Happy* (even though that did go to #1 in 1988 for Bobby McFerrin), but you get the idea.

Song Titles

- The Babysitter Said I Had to Go to Bed
- I Can See Between the Cracks of Your Lies
- My Heart Goes Boom
- Liberty Avenue
- Fools Like Me

Chord Progression for a Song
C-G-Am-G (I-V-vi-V)

Word Association Exercises

_____ And Sundays   Life Is Like A _____

_____ Girls And _____ Boys   Secrets I've _____

Old As _____   _____ Sanctuary

Songwriters Hall of Fame: Michael Jackson

Hall of Fame Induction: 2002. Regardless of what people might think about Michael Jackson as a controversial personality or person, there is little dispute about his qualities as a top-of-the-chart songwriter. He began his music career at the age of seven with The Jackson 5 and has since racked up 13 Grammy awards and released 13 #1 singles in the U.S. His monumental *Thriller* album is the second best-selling album of all time. **Little known fact:** Jackson owns half of Sony/ATV Music Publishing which owns most of the Lennon/McCartney song catalog. He outbid Paul McCartney for those rights. McCartney never forgave Jackson as it was McCartney who told him about the investment value of song catalogs in the first place. **Recommended listening:** *Thriller, Bad* and *Off The Wall*.

"I find that the harder I work, the more luck I seem to have." --
Thomas Jefferson

Inspirational Quote

An Idea to Write a Song About

You are cleaning out the attic or garage and trying to get rid of what seems to be an incredible amount of junk. It's hard parting with some of the items as there are so many memories attached. You finally come across a torn and tattered teddy bear you rarely parted with as a child...

Note Sequence for a Song
G-A-B♭-A-B♭-F-G

Power Words
Silence / Jungle / Demon / Leather / Straw

Cliches, Expressions, Slang and Idioms
• Light at the end of the tunnel
• Fighting to the bitter end
• With every tick of the clock

Rolling Stone Magazine's Greatest Songs of all Time -- #19
HOUND DOG (Elvis Presley) 1956 (Songwriters: Leiber/Stoller)
A FEW LINES: "You ain't nothin' but a hound dog. / Cryin' all the time. / You ain't nothin' but a hound dog. / Cryin' all the time. / Well, you ain't never caught a rabbit. / And you ain't no friend of mine."
DID YOU KNOW... The first version of this Leiber/Stoller song was released by Big Mama Thornton in 1953 and hit #1 on the R&B charts. Elvis Presley heard the song being performed while in Vegas in 1956. He recorded his version the same year and it sold over 4 million copies in its first release.

Songwriter's Toolkit
Roget's 21st Century Thesaurus (Dell)
by Barbara Ann Kipfer (ISBN: 044024269X)
This thesaurus provides a simple, reliable way to find the perfect word. It features an easy-to-use dictionary format plus a revolutionary Concept Index that arranges words by idea. It includes a wide variety of words and phrases with each entry fitting any variation of style and tone. ($5.99)

Songwriter Quote

"I thought I knew a lot about music. Then you start digging and the deeper you go, the more there is." -- ***John Mellencamp***

SUNDAY

MONDAY

TUESDAY

WEDNESDAY

THURSDAY

FRIDAY

SATURDAY

Songwriting Exercise

This exercise is similar to the "free association" used earlier in this book. This time write a "power word" in the center of a sheet of paper. (Use one of the "power words" in this book or choose one of your own.) Circle it and then think of a word that relates to it. Write this word down, circle it and draw a line between the two words. Now think of another word which relates to either your original word or the new word. Write it down, circle it and connect the two words. Continue the exercise connecting any of the words on the page. When you are done you will find a distinct pattern of words that suggests a great song title, idea or hook. (This is also known as "webbing".)

Song Titles

- Your Pet Pig Is Dead (Please Pass Me A Porkchop)
- When Push Comes to Shove
- Death Is Easy (Life Is Hard)
- Haunted Hallways
- Visits From Venus

Chord Progression for a Song
Am-D-Em (i-IV-v)

Word Association Exercises

_____ And Frilly

Along The _____

Azure _____

On The Road To _____

Mood, Music And _____

_____ And Silhouettes

Songwriters Hall of Fame: Jimmy Webb

Hall of Fame Induction: 1986. Although Webb has always performed his own music, it is the dozens of songs recorded by others that made him a huge success as a songwriter. Between 1966 and 1969 alone, he was responsible for writing such platinum-selling classics as *By the Time I Get to Phoenix, Wichita Lineman, Up Up and Away* and *MacArthur Park*. **Little known fact:** Jimmy Webb is the only person to receive Grammy Awards in all three categories: music, lyrics and orchestration. **Recommended listening:** *Words and Music, Ten Easy Pieces* and *Twilight of the Renegades*.

"The artist is nothing without the gift, but the gift is nothing without work." **-- Emile Zola**

Inspirational Quote

An Idea to Write a Song About
You are a grasshopper just merrily hopping through the grass minding your own business. You wouldn't mind finding some of that delicious lettuce across the yard in the vegetable garden. But suddenly you hear a sound. The sound of a lawnmower headed your direction...

Note Sequence for a Song
E-E-E-D-G-F-E

Power Words
Ramble / Tenement / Shelter / Priest / Boulevard

Cliches, Expressions, Slang and Idioms
- A faint heart never won a maiden fair
- Back in the brown shoe days
- Dead in the water

Rolling Stone Magazine's Greatest Songs of all Time -- #20
LET IT BE (The Beatles) 1970 (Songwriters: Lennon/McCartney)
A FEW LINES: "When I find myself in times of trouble. / Mother Mary comes to me. / Speaking words of wisdom, let it be. / And in my hour of darkness. / She is standing right in front of me. / Speaking words of wisdom, let it be."
DID YOU KNOW... Many people thought this song was a biblical reference when it was released. It was actually a tribute to Paul McCartney's mother who died when he was 14 years old.

Songwriter's Toolkit
Yamaha YPT-200 Keyboard
If you're looking for in inexpensive keyboard that still delivers everything you need, this one might be it. First you have a selection of 134 digitally-sampled voices to deliver authentic sounds of different instruments. Then there are 100 selectable accompaniment styles. With a built-in teaching device, the keyboard also offers step-by-step instruction to would-be musicians. As an entry-level keyboard, the YPT-200 is a fine instrument for aspiring musicians. ($100)

"Anything can inspire me - a conversation, something strikes you about words which can end up being a title." -- Barry Gibb

SUNDAY

MONDAY

TUESDAY

WEDNESDAY

THURSDAY

FRIDAY

SATURDAY

Songwriting Exercise

I know I've provided many cliches in this book, but the bottom line is, unless a cliche is your song title or hook, cliches should be "avoided like the plague". They "shouldn't be touched with a ten foot pole". They should... well, you get the idea. They are easier to "get away with" if they are the central theme of your song, but make sure they haven't been used (or over-used) before. Bob Seeger had a great hit with *Like A Rock*, but you probably wouldn't want to use it again. So take out a few of your finished songs and search for cliches. When you find one, change it up. Make it original. Make it your own!

Song Titles

- Tangled Tumbleweeds
- If The Sun Don't Shine, It Ain't My Fault
- A Walk In The Willows
- (We Are) Living In The Dark Ages
- Old Girlfriends Are Like Boomerangs

Chord Progression for a Song
C-Am-F-G (I-vi-IV-V)

Word Association Exercises

More _____ Than _____   Highways And _____

Just A Bag Of _____   Complicated By _____

_____ In The Street   A Handful Of _____

Songwriters Hall of Fame: Glenn Frey

Hall of Fame Induction: 2000. Beginning with members of a band backing up Linda Ronstadt on tour, The Eagles became one of the greatest bands in rock history. Along with Don Henley, Frey wrote or co-wrote many of their hits. He also made his niche as a solo artist with *The Heat Is On* from Beverly Hills Cop and *You Belong In The City.* **Little known fact:** Frey's first professional recording experience was playing guitar and singing background vocals on Bob Seger's *Ramblin' Gamblin' Man* in 1968. **Recommended listening:** *Desperado, Hotel California* and *Glenn Frey Live.*

---

*"The secret of good writing is to say an old thing in a new way or to say a new thing in an old way." -- **Richard Harding Davis***

Inspirational Quote

An Idea to Write a Song About

You open weary eyes as if from a fretful sleep or a dream you can't quite remember. You look around and see similarly dressed people standing in a row on both sides of you. Behind you there's a knight on a horse and, yes, that looks like a king and a queen back there. That's when you realize you are a pawn on a chessboard and it's your turn to move...

Note Sequence for a Song

B-G-A-F#-G-E-D

Power Words

Whimper / Electric / Gladiator / Queen / Revival

Cliches, Expressions, Slang and Idioms

- Cut me some slack
- Zero is sometimes better than nothing
- A monkey in silk is a monkey no less

Rolling Stone Magazine's Greatest Songs of all Time -- #21

BORN TO RUN (Bruce Springsteen) 1975 (Songwriter: Springsteen)
A FEW LINES: "Baby this town rips the bones from your back. / It's a death trap, it's a suicide rap. / We gotta get out while we're young. / 'Cause tramps like us, baby we were born to run."
DID YOU KNOW... This song came at a crossroads in Springsteen's career. His first two albums had sold poorly and it was rumored that Columbia Records was ready to drop him if he didn't produce a hit.

Songwriter's Toolkit

Pandora Internet Radio (pandora.com)
Wouldn't it be nice if you could have your own personal radio station that only played the types of music you enjoyed? Well, the future is here. At Pandora Internet Radio you enter your favorite songs and musicians and establish a radio station personalized just for you. Sound too good to be true? Then check it out at pandora.com.

*"I take notes all the time, too. You know, something terrible happens to you, and you think, 'Bastards. I'm going to write a song about that.' And then you do." -- **Richard Thompson***

SUNDAY

MONDAY

TUESDAY

WEDNESDAY

THURSDAY

FRIDAY

SATURDAY

Songwriting Exercise

Take out a pen and paper and make a list of ten things that bother you. The list can consist of the small, irritating things in your life (like standing in line at the grocery store or receiving 38 e-mails about improving your love life) or more important things (like global warming or taxes). Once you have created your list, sit down and see if any of the ideas are strong enough to convey images of a song.

Song Titles

- Billy Went To War, But He Didn't Come Home
- Awful Waffles, Achin' For Bacon
- Blessed Are The Geeks
- Umbrellas Never Opened
- The Future Smiles On Laughing Souls

Chord Progression for a Song
C-F-D-G (I-IV-II-V)

Word Association Exercises

The Joy Of _____

Standing By The _____

Prayer For The _____

Dreaming Of _____

Pages Of _____

Blue As _____

Songwriters Hall of Fame: Curtis Mayfield

Hall of Fame Induction: 2000. Most people recognize the name Curtis Mayfield even if they don't remember he was a member of *The Impressions*. And even though he was known as a singer, he was also the primary songwriter for the group. He was also among the first in his profession to speak openly about African-American pride and community struggle in his compositions. He triumphed through many personal tragedies in the 1990's (he was paralyzed from the neck down after an onstage accident in 1990) and passed away in 1999. **Little known fact:** The Impressions were originally called The Roosters. **Recommended listening:** *Freddie's Dead, Back to the World* and *The Anthology: 1961-1977.*

"Writing isn't hard. It isn't any harder than ditch-digging."
-- Patrick Dennis

An Idea to Write a Song About

You're a dog living a dog's life. Everything is great. You get the run of the backyard and even occasionally escape to roam the neighborhood. You always have food and water handy and even manage to grab an occasional table scrap from one of the kids. Yes, everything is fine. Until the new pet cat arrives...

Note Sequence for a Song
D-G-E-A-F#-E-G

Power Words
Piazza / Stallion / Pilgrim / Brittle / Tumble

Cliches, Expressions, Slang and Idioms
- Spinning like a top
- You only live once, but once should be enough
- As nervous as a virgin at a prison rodeo

Rolling Stone Magazine's Greatest Songs of all Time -- #22
BE MY BABY (The Ronettes) 1963 (Songwriters: Barry/Greenwich/Spector)
A FEW LINES: "I'll make you happy, baby. / Just wait and see. / For every kiss you give me. / I'll give you three."
DID YOU KNOW... Cher sang backup vocals on the production. She was working for producer Phil Spector at the time. Spector later married (then divorced) Ronnie Bennet, one of The Ronettes.

Songwriter's Toolkit
The Definitive Bob Dylan Songbook (Amsco Music)
Any serious songwriter should not be without a songbook containing Bob Dylan tunes. This one fits the bill and features over 329 tunes, including all of his greatest hits as well as lesser known works. *Blowin' In the Wind, Just Like A Woman, Mr. Tambourine Man, She Belongs to Me* and hundreds more are included. Even if you are a songwriter who doesn't play an instrument you should own this book just to study the lyrics. (ISBN: 082561774X) ($39.95)

*"Every now and then you'll nail one that's really, really special. And that's what you live for." -- **Bob Seger***

SUNDAY

MONDAY

TUESDAY

WEDNESDAY

THURSDAY

FRIDAY

SATURDAY

Songwriting Exercise

Write a song with a question as the title such as *Who'll Stop The Rain?, Will You Love Me Tomorrow?* or *Where Have All The Flowers Gone?* are some examples. The song can either build on the question and answer it by building toward the end or answer the question in the chorus. Of course, you don't have to answer the question at all.

Song Titles

- Flying Down The Highway With The Highbeams On
- Style Without Grace
- Second Thoughts For The Third Time
- Shallow As Me
- Ten After Two (And Still Waiting For You)

Chord Progression for a Song
    C-Am-Dm-F (I-vi-ii-IV)

Word Association Exercises

Crying Like A _____   _____ And Windows

Hold Onto Your _____   _____ In Pigtails

Painting Pictures Of _____   Over The _____

Songwriters Hall of Fame: Elton John/Bernie Taupin

Hall of Fame Induction: 1992. Match the melodic songwriting skills of Elton John with the magical lyrics of Bernie Taupin and the rest is history. John became one of the dominant forces in the rock world during the '70s with a string of seven consecutive #1 albums on the U.S. charts, 23 Top 40 singles, 16 Top 10 hits and six singles hitting #1. The songwriting duo also has five Grammy awards to their credit. **Little known fact:** After failing at an audition, Elton John was given several song lyrics written by Taupin. Although they started writing songs together (corresponding by mail), they didn't meet until six months later. **Recommended listening:** *Don't Shoot Me I'm Only the Piano Player, Goodbye Yellow Brick Road* and *Captain Fantastic And The Brown Dirt Cowboy.*

"The man who makes no mistakes does not usually make anything."
-- Bishop W.C. Magee

Inspirational Quote

An Idea to Write a Song About

Write a song about snack foods. Licorice, gum drops, Twinkies. Any scrumptious snack you can imagine. Do you love them? Hate them? Do you avoid them as much as possible or do you long for them every moment of the day?

Note Sequence for a Song
A-A-C-C-B-B-D

Power Words
Gingerbread / Venus / Fingers / Amazing / Village

Cliches, Expressions, Slang and Idioms
• Harmony in disharmony
• Back to square one
• Hot as a pistol, cold as death

Rolling Stone Magazine's Greatest Songs of all Time -- #23
In My Life (The Beatles) 1965 (Songwriters: Lennon/McCartney)
A FEW LINES: "Though I know I'll never lose affection. / For people and things that went before. / I know I'll often stop and think about them. / In my life, I love you more."
DID YOU KNOW... The Beatles left room for an instrumental break when they recorded this. Producer George Martin filled it with a piano solo and made it sound like a harpsichord by speeding up the tape.

Songwriter's Toolkit
Tunesmith: Inside the Art of Songwriting (Hyperion)
by Jimmy Webb (ISBN: 0786884886)
Recording artist and songwriter Jimmy Webb brings his insider knowledge and experience to a solid guide for aspiring songwriters. With a combination of anecdotes, meditation and advice, Webb breaks down the creative process of songwriting from beginning to end, from coping with writers block to song construction, chord, and even self-promotion. Webb also gives readers a glimpse into the world of professional music. ($15.95)

Songwriter Quote

"You could write about some kind of emotional problem you are having, but it would not be a good song, in my eyes, until it went through a period of sensitivity to a moment of clarity. Without that moment of clarity... it's just complaining." -- Joni Mitchell

SUNDAY

MONDAY

TUESDAY

WEDNESDAY

THURSDAY

FRIDAY

SATURDAY

Songwriting Exercise

If you have a keyboard, sit down and play around with a sequence of notes. Don't try to play any accompanying chords, just hit a series of random notes until something clicks and says "Hey, I sound good. Use me!". You can also use a guitar or other instrument, but I've found the keyboard works best for this exercise. Don't have a keyboard? Type in the keywords "virtual keyboard" and you'll find several online "instruments" that you can experiment with.

Song Titles

- Dogs And Cats In Black Top Hats
- Are Your Thoughts Worth More Than A Penny?
- Did You See Which Way Love Went?
- Everybody Thinks They're Better, But They Ain't
- Crossbeams

Chord Progression for a Song
C-A♭-B♭-F (I-VI♭-VII♭-IV)

Word Association Exercises

A _____ Kind Of Love   Starlight And _____

_____ And Mysteries   _____ And Lazy

Beauty As Shallow As _____   And The _____ Will Follow

Songwriters Hall of Fame: Brian Wilson

Hall of Fame Induction: 2000. Brian Wilson began his musical career with The Beach Boys, of which he was a founding member, bassist, main producer, composer, arranger and sometimes lead singer. Brian left the group in 1967 although he continued to write songs and produced their albums. After years of dealing with depression and drugs, Wilson met with limited success as a solo artist. **Little known fact:** Wilson did not like recording in stereo sound as he believed it gave an incomplete "sound picture" if the listener wasn't directly between the speakers. **Recommended listening:** *Pet Sounds, Endless Summer* and *SMile*.

"We would accomplish many more things if we did not think of them as impossible." -- *C. Malesherbes*

Inspirational Quote

An Idea to Write a Song About

There have been many songs written about the wind. (*Summer Wind, Blowin' in the Wind, Wayward Wind*). But how about a song written from the perspective of the wind?

Note Sequence for a Song
A-B-C-D-E-F-E

Power Words
Charlatan / Adobe / Stagger / Death / Scuffle

Cliches, Expressions, Slang and Idioms
- Captain of his soul
- As every schoolboy knows
- On the spur of the moment

Rolling Stone Magazine's Greatest Songs of all Time -- #24
PEOPLE GET READY (The Impressions) 1965
(Songwriter: Curtis Mayfield)
A FEW LINES: "People get ready, there's a train comin'. / You don't need no baggage, you just get on board. / All you need is faith to hear the diesels hummin'. / You don't need no ticket you just thank the Lord."
DID YOU KNOW... Shortly after *People Get Ready* was released, Chicago churches began including their own version of it in their songbooks.

Songwriter's Toolkit
Garage Band (Mac only)
To put it simply, this may be the best bang for the buck on the market. The program combines the CD-quality samples of Apple's Soundtrack with the hard-disk recording features of *Digital Performer* and the canned rhythm tracks of *Band in a Box*. But what's really amazing is the way this program can turn inspiration into commercial-sounding demos. Imagine how thousands of musicians, though blessed with creative talent, remain undiscovered because they lack the resources they need. For them, *GarageBand* may open a lot of doors -- or just offer a lot of fun. (Included with Apple's iLife package/$79.00)

Songwriter Quote

"My songs are just little letters to me." -- Ani DiFranco

SUNDAY

MONDAY

TUESDAY

WEDNESDAY

THURSDAY

FRIDAY

SATURDAY

Songwriting Exercise

A good percentage of songs are written in 4/4 time. So change it up. Choose a key and set up a nice 3/4 (waltz) tempo. If you have a drum machine or a percussion program built into your keyboard, use it, but it's pretty easy to set up the rhythm without one. 1-2-3. 1-2-3. 1-2-3. And away we go!

Song Titles

- Happy Hour At The Zombie Bar
- Feeding The Buzzards
- Don't They Provide Warranties For Marriages In Vegas?
- It's Like Living In The Vacuum Of Space
- Heavy As Helium

Chord Progression for a Song
Am-F-C-G (i-VI-III-VII)

Word Association Exercises

Nights Without _____

A State Of _____

Tears Rolling Like _____

Once In A _____

Blue Jeans And _____

Just _____ Me

Songwriters Hall of Fame: Eric Clapton

Hall of Fame Induction: 2001. Although Clapton has only one #1 single to his credit (*I Shot the Sheriff*), he is the only person inducted into the Rock and Roll Hall of Fame three times. He was inducted as a member of the Yardbirds in 1992, Cream in 1993 and as a solo artist in 2000. As a solo artist and a member of these groups, Clapton had seven albums listed in Rolling Stone's "500 Greatest Albums of All Time." He also has 16 Grammy Awards to his name. **Little known fact:** When George Harrison walked out during a recording session in 1969 for the Beatles' *Let It Be* album, John Lennon (fearing that Harrison was gone for good) proposed that Harrison be replaced by Clapton. **Recommended listening:** *Unplugged* and *Slowhand* (solo albums), *Layla and Other Assorted Love Songs* (Derek and the Dominos) and *Disraeli Gears* (Cream).

"A ship in harbor is safe -- but that is not what ships are built for."
-- John A. Shedd

Inspirational Quote

An Idea to Write a Song About

Write a song from the perspective of a rock in the middle of a stream. The years and decades pass as the water continues to pound at you. Is the song positive as you've lasted this long or negative as the water is taking its toll?

Note Sequence for a Song
F-B♭-F-F-C-G-B♭-F

Power Words
Bungalow / Horizon / Penthouse / Manuscript / Glitter

Cliches, Expressions, Slang and Idioms
- Stone cold sober
- In the land of the blind, the one-eyed man is king
- Beauty is only a light switch away

Rolling Stone Magazine's Greatest Songs of all Time -- #25
GOD ONLY KNOWS (The Beach Boys) 1966 (Songwriters: Wilson/Asher)
A FEW LINES: "I may not always love you. / But long as there are stars above you. / You never need to doubt it. / I'll make you so sure about it. / God only knows what I'd be without you."
DID YOU KNOW... Paul McCartney and John Lennon first heard this on The Beach Boys' *Pet Sounds* album. Influenced heavily by this cut, they went back to McCartney's house and wrote *Here, There and Everywhere*.

Songwriter's Toolkit
Successful Lyric Writing (Writer's Digest Books)
by Sheila Davis (ISBN: 0898792835)
This book presents a series of exercises, practice critiques and quizzes that reinforce songwriting theory and prepares songwriters for the main feature of the book -- ten specially-designed lyric-writing assignments. Davis concludes the course by teaching songwriters to expand their songwriting abilities on their own and realize their potential. The book provides everything songwriters need to take their talent to the limit. ($22.95)

"If you're going to come away from a party singing the lyrics of a song, it is better that you sing of self-pride like 'We're a Winner' instead of 'Do the Boo-ga-loo!'" -- **Curtis Mayfield**

SUNDAY

MONDAY

TUESDAY

WEDNESDAY

THURSDAY

FRIDAY

SATURDAY

Songwriting Exercise

You'll need to do this exercise when you have several hours of free time. It is similar to the "write a song in ten minutes" exercise, but this time you will write ten songs in one day. Now remember, the object is to write ten different songs. They don't all have to be "works of art", just see if you can write ten of them in a day. Then let them "age" for a few days and go back and take a look and see what you have. You might be surprised. If nothing else you'll always be able to brag about the fact that you wrote ten songs in a single day!

Song Titles
- Plans I Should Have Made
- Like Ice Cream And Candy
- Sneakers Aren't Just For Sneakin' (He Said As He Was Running)
- An Ordinary Celebration
- Knowing Everything Is A Little Like Knowing Nothing At All

Chord Progression for a Song
C-F-A♭-Gm (I-IV-VI♭-v)

Word Association Exercises

_____ Reflections   Mountain Of _____

The Monkey And The _____   Fancy _____

_____ Days And _____ Nights   _____ Highways

Songwriters Hall of Fame: Dolly Parton

Hall of Fame Induction: 2001. It might be hard to find a performer who moved so smoothly from her country roots to international stardom than Dolly Parton. By the age of ten she was already performing professionally on both television and radio. When her hit song *Here You Come Again* crossed over successfully to the pop charts, she said "I'm not leaving county music. I'm just taking it with me." **Little known fact:** The first cloned mammal was a sheep named "Dolly" in honor of Parton because it was cloned from a mammary cell. **Recommended listening:** *Here You Come Again, Eagle When She Flies* and *The Grass Is Blue.*

"Writers have two main problems. One is writer's block, when the words won't come at all, and the other is logorrhea, when the words come so fast that they can hardly get to the wastebasket in time." -- *Cecelia Bartholomew*

An Idea to Write a Song About

You're out on a date. It's been a great evening. You're sitting on the couch making small talk, hoping for a little more. But your date just keeps talking and talking and talking...

Note Sequence for a Song
C-G-E-G-C-G-E

Power Words
Ancient / Blazing / Ebony / Claws / Rough

Cliches, Expressions, Slang and Idioms
- Falling between the cracks
- Too close for comfort
- Pay the fiddler if you want to dance

Rolling Stone Magazine's Greatest Songs of all Time -- #26
A SAY IN THE LIFE (The Beatles) 1967 (Songwriters: Lennon/McCartney)
A FEW LINES: "I saw a film today, oh boy. / The English army had just won the war. / A crowd of people turned away. / But I just had to look. / Having read the book. / I'd love to turn you on."
DID YOU KNOW... The final chord in the song was created by all 4 Beatles and George Martin banging on 3 pianos simultaneously. The final note lasts 42 seconds.

McGill English Dictionary of Rhyme (BryantMcGill.com)
Rhyming Software for Windows 95/98/Me/NT/2000/XP/2003
Whether you re a poet, a rapper or a marketing writer, there will come a time when inspiration leaves you. This is where this book can help. You simply enter a word in the search box and the application instantly displays rhyming terms in one of three columns. The first column is for standard, straight-up rhymes; the second is for rhyming phrases; and the third is for Roundex rhymes (words that sound similar but don't actually rhyme.) And the best part about this software is that it doesn't cost a dime! (Free)

"Being a good songwriter means paying attention and sticking your hand out the window to catch the song on the way to someone else's house!" -- Nanci Griffith

SUNDAY

MONDAY

TUESDAY

WEDNESDAY

THURSDAY

FRIDAY

SATURDAY

Songwriting Exercise

This exercise is long-term, but I guarantee it will pay off eventually. The idea here is to learn as many "cover" songs as you can. Find a song that you like and learn how to play it. Buy CDs and songbooks or download songs online. Many songs have chords and/or tablature available online as well. The more songs you learn, the better your songwriting will become.

Song Titles

- Klingons In The Closet
- She's No Angel, But She's Heaven On Earth
- The Bells Don't Chime And The Chimes Don't Ring
- Spies In The Spotlight
- Final Frontiers Are Never Really Final

Chord Progression for a Song
C-F-D♭-G (I-IV-II♭-V)

Word Association Exercises

_____ Dreams

_____ Eyes

Floating On A _____

_____ In The House

Broken _____

Visions Of _____

Songwriters Hall of Fame: Barry Manilow

Hall of Fame Induction: 2002. For many people the name Barry Manilow does not seem synonymous with the term great songwriter, but the facts reveal a different story. Among his 31 albums are 38 Top 40 hits. Ironically, even though Manilow has written scores of songs over the years, most of his major hits were written by others. He was able to secure his own record deal in 1973 after working for two years as Bette Midler's pianist, arranger and musical conductor. **Little known fact:** Early in his career, Manilow was a commercial jingle writer/singer. He wrote the theme music for State Farm Insurance ("Like a Good Neighbor") and the "Stuck on Band-Aid" jingle among many others. **Recommended listening:** *I Write The Songs, This One's For You* and *Tryin' to Get the Feeling.*

An Idea to Write a Song About

There is a box sitting in the center of the dining room table. It has no name or address on it. So, what's in the box? Where did it come from? Who did it come from?

Note Sequence for a Song
E-E-A-G-E-B-E

Power Words
Passion / Casket / Squiggle / Waterfall / Tapestry

Cliches, Expressions, Slang and Idioms
- Hell bent and heaven bound
- Feeling bad is just a new sensation
- Weaving tales

Rolling Stone Magazine's Greatest Songs of all Time -- #27
LAYLA (Derek and the Dominos) 1970 (Songwriters: Clapton/Gordon)
A FEW LINES: "What'll you do when you get lonely. / And nobody's waitin' by your side. / You've been runnin' and hidin' much too long. / You know it's just your foolish pride. / Layla, you got me on my knees. / Layla, I'm beggin' darlin', please. / Layla, darlin', won't you ease my worried mind."
DID YOU KNOW... The lyrics to this song are based on a book by Persian poet Nizami titled "Layla and Majnun" about a man in love with a woman who cannot have her because her parents object.

Songwriter's Toolkit
Essential Songwriter's Rhyming Dictionary (Alfred Publishing Company) by Kevin M. Mitchell (ISBN: 0882847295)
Acclaimed by the *New York Times* as "part muse, part quick reference," this pocket-sized dictionary is an easy-to-use tool geared specifically toward the contemporary songwriter. It is a concise collection of the most-often used words in popular music. The simple format allows for fast reference, while the 15,000 entries provide more than ample rhyming options. ($5.95)

"I didn't choose a word or anything. I just wrote the song until it stopped." -- Marty Robbins

SUNDAY

MONDAY

TUESDAY

WEDNESDAY

THURSDAY

FRIDAY

SATURDAY

Songwriting Exercise

Driving through rush hour with nothing to do? Taking a long, leisurely shower? Making dinner? Do a little multi-tasking and sing while you're doing something else. Make up new, nonsensical lyrics. Develop a new tune. It's these opportunities that sometimes free up the mind and allows you to discover the beginnings of a great new tune.

Song Titles

- A Million Thorns, A Single Rose
- Window Pane Rain
- Anyone Can Be A Hero On Halloween
- Buy Me A Ticket To Mars
- Peaches And Dreams

Chord Progression for a Song
Am-F-G-Am (i-VIb-VIIb-i)

Word Association Exercises

Changes In _____   Blind _____

_____ Light   Hope And _____

Smoke And _____   _____ Talk

Songwriters Hall of Fame: Willie Nelson

Hall of Fame Induction: 2001. Willie Nelson's songwriting career and musical career had many ups and downs in the early years. Early on he split time between performing and being a radio disc jockey. Even after a string of hits including *Hello Walls* (Farron Young) and *Crazy* (Patsy Cline), his career ground to a halt. But a dozen years later found him recording *Red Headed Stranger* and his career was established for good. **Little known fact:** Nelson sold a song early in his career called *Family Bible*. The song was a hit for Claude Gray in 1960. It has been covered widely and is often considered a gospel music classic. Nelson sold the song for $50. **Recommended listening:** *Always On My Mind, Stardust* and *Waylon and Willie*.

"I find that the harder I work, the more luck I seem to have."
-- *Thomas Jefferson*

Inspirational Quote

An Idea to Write a Song About
What if you could fly? What would it feel like to soar above the clouds? And how would you describe it in song?

Note Sequence for a Song
G-G-A-A-C-B-A

Power Words
Flutter / Chuckle / Wicked / Cotton / Melt

Cliches, Expressions, Slang and Idioms
• There is harmony in disharmony
• Midnight is where the day begins
• Truth is nothing but a feeling that something is true

Rolling Stone Magazine's Greatest Songs of all Time -- #28
DOCK OF THE BAY (Otis Redding) 1968 (Songwriters: Redding/Cropper)
A FEW LINES: "Sitting in the morning sun. / I'll be sitting when the evening comes. / Watching the ships roll in. / Then I watch them roll away again. / I'm sitting on the dock of the bay. / Watching the tide roll away. / I'm just sitting on the dock of the bay. / Wasting time."
DID YOU KNOW... Redding hadn't written a last verse to this when he recorded it, so he whistled instead. He planned to return to Memphis and fill in the verse later, but he died in a plane crash before he had the chance.

Songwriter's Toolkit
Alesis SR16 Drum Machine
As one of the most popular drum machines ever made, the SR-16 has been used by everyone from songwriters to live performers to remix engineers as their drum machine of choice. The reason is simple: it features a great selection of 233 realistic, natural drum sounds, offered both in dry form and sampled with digital reverbs. The SR-16 features 50 preset patterns that were actually played by top studio drummers, not just programmed and quantized. ($149.00)

Songwriter Quote

"When I start writing songs and it turns into an overly belabored intellectual process, I just throw it out." -- *Alanis Morissette*

SUNDAY

MONDAY

TUESDAY

WEDNESDAY

THURSDAY

FRIDAY

SATURDAY

Songwriting Exercise

This one ought to be fun. No matter what decade we've lived in there were always dance tunes being written that become wildly popular. Even youngsters know there was a dance in the 60's called the Twist. Or the country-western craze known as the Electric Slide in the 80's. And even as recently as the 90's the Macarena swept the entire world. So write the next dance song. Find yourself a rhythm you could dance to, add some words that conjure some type of dance movement and have some fun!

Song Titles

- Cruisin' In My Corvette
- Katie Klondike
- Love Ain't Blind (It's Only Near-Sighted)
- Cellular Blues
- Why Keep Lying When The Truth Don't Matter?

Chord Progression for a Song
C-F-B♭-F (I-IV-VIIb-IV)

Word Association Exercises

Holes In My _____   The Theory Of _____

Like A _____ In A Graveyard   Journey To _____

The Dark _____ Of _____   Music Of The _____

Songwriters Hall of Fame: Sting

Hall of Fame Induction: 2002. Sting formed The Police when he was in his early twenties and never looked back. The Police, with Sting as lead singer, bassist and principal composer, had nine Top 40 hits in the U.S. including *Every Breath You Take* which remained at #1 one for 8 weeks. He continued his success after leaving the band with hit singles and award-winning albums. He has also become known as an environmental and human rights activist. **Little known fact:** Sting is said to have been the inspiration for the character John Constantine in the "Hellblazer" comic books and movie. **Recommended listening:** *Synchronicity, Ten Summoner's Tales* and *Brand New Day.*

*"Motivation is what gets you started. Habit is what keeps you going." -- **Jim Ryun***

Inspirational Quote

An Idea to Write a Song About
You've had a great day at the county fair. Three bags of popcorn, two tacos, three hot dogs, steak on a stick, two funnel cakes and five beers later you think you might have had enough...

Note Sequence for a Song
E-A-E-A-E-C-B-A

Power Words
Shadow / Mist / Candlestick / Voodoo / Mystic

Cliches, Expressions, Slang and Idioms
• The truth is just as meaningful as the lie
• Nothing for free
• Winners need their losers

Rolling Stone Magazine's Greatest Songs of all Time -- #29
HELP! (The Beatles) 1965 (Songwriters: Lennon/McCartney)
A FEW LINES: "When I was younger, so much younger than today. / I never needed anybody's help in any way. / But now those days are gone, I'm not so self assured. / Now I find I've changed my mind and opened up the doors."
DID YOU KNOW... This became the first Beatles song ever used in a commercial when Ford used it in 1985. The company paid $100,000 for it although the version in the commercial was performed by a sound-alike group.

Songwriter's Toolkit
Lyricist (Virtual Studio Systems) virtualstudiosystems.com
Software for Win95, Win98, Win2000, WinME, WinNT, WinXP
Lyricist is the ultimate songwriting tool. No more folders full of unorganized document files. No more searching through the pages of your rhyming dictionary or scanning the thesaurus for just the right word. *Lyricist* combines everything you need for lyric writing and archiving into one package. You'd be hard-pressed to find another program that incorporates so many essential features for the songwriter. ($49.95)

"I guess you could write a good song if your heart hadn't been broken, but I don't know of anyone whose heart hasn't been broken."
-- Lucinda Williams

SUNDAY

MONDAY

TUESDAY

WEDNESDAY

THURSDAY

FRIDAY

SATURDAY

Songwriting Exercise

The next time you are at an art show or visiting the museum, find a painting that you really enjoy. With pen and paper in hand, create a story behind the painting. Not how the painting was created, but what inspired the painting or simply what story the painting tells you. Take those notes home and write the song. (You can also surf through paintings online and do the exercise that way.) Another exercise you can do is to write down a few names of paintings and use them for song titles.

Song Titles

- The Dead Just Lie Around And Frown
- Bending The Rules, But Breaking Her Heart
- Crossing Yellow Lines
- Collectible Kisses
- If Love Was Science, I'd Flunk For Sure

Chord Progression for a Song
C-Dm-F-G (I-ii-IV-V)

Word Association Exercises

_____ And Pennies

Me And _____

A Heart Full Of _____

Faces In The _____

_____ And Modesty

Baskets Of _____

Songwriters Hall of Fame: Bob Dylan

Hall of Fame Induction: 1982. With 50 albums to his name, Bob Dylan is one of the most recorded songwriters of the modern rock era. He has been inducted into the Nashville Songwriters Hall of Fame as well as the Rock and Roll Hall of Fame. He has 8 Grammy awards to his credit and has even been nominated several times for the Nobel Prize in Literature. **Little known fact:** When Dylan released his *Modern Times* album in 2006, it became his first #1 album in the U.S. in thirty years. It also made him the oldest living person (65) to top the charts. **Recommended listening:** *Bringing It All Back Home*, *Blonde On Blonde* and *Blood On The Tracks*.

*"I've missed more than 9,000 shots in my career. I've lost more than 300 games. Twenty-six times I've been trusted to take the game-winning shot and missed. I've failed over and over and over again in my life... And that is why I succeed." -- **Michael Jordan***

Inspirational Quote

An Idea to Write a Song About

Are dogs and cats really enemies? Write a song from the perspective of either a cat or a dog on this subject.

Note Sequence for a Song
A-F-A-F-E-F-A-G

Power Words

Shock / Shiver / Icicle / Champagne / Snowflake

Cliches, Expressions, Slang and Idioms

- It'll feel better when it stops hurting
- We are all alone
- Better the devil you know than the devil you don't

Rolling Stone Magazine's Greatest Songs of all Time -- #30

I WALK THE LINE (Johnny Cash) 1956 (Songwriter: Cash)

A FEW LINES: "I keep a close watch on this heart of mine. / I keep my eyes wide open all the time. / I keep the ends out for the tie that binds. / Because you're mine, I walk the line."

DID YOU KNOW... The original version of this song uses a key change between each of the verses with Cash humming the new root note before singing each verse. The unique chord progression was inspired by an accidental backwards playback on Cash's tape recorder while he was in the Air Force.

Songwriter's Toolkit

Sing Out! Published (4 times a year)

Sing Out! covers all types of folk music including world music, Celtic, blues, ballads, Cajun music, singer-songwriters, bluegrass, storytelling, political songs, children's music, and much more. Each issue includes lead sheets for 20 or more traditional and contemporary folk songs, plus in-depth feature articles and interviews, instrumental teach-ins, tons of recording and book reviews, a comprehensive and up-to-date folk festival listing and regular columns on the folk process, songwriting and more. ($6.95/single issue or $25/year)

"When I'm inspired, I get excited because I can't wait to see what I'll come up with next." -- ***Dolly Parton***

SUNDAY

MONDAY

TUESDAY

WEDNESDAY

THURSDAY

FRIDAY

SATURDAY

Songwriting Exercise

Write the chorus to a song, but keep the number of words in the chorus to 12 words or less. You can repeat words, of course, but you can't go over 12. The idea here is to focus on a single idea for your song and not get carried away at this point with too many lyrics. It will also help you focus on a solid hook, the heartbeat behind every song.

Song Titles

- Like Rabbits In A Rodeo
- Like An Open Book
- A Forest Without Trees
- Olive Oyl And Popeye Got Married In Mexico
- Fading Memories

Chord Progression for a Song
Am-G-F-E (i-VII-VI-V)

Word Association Exercises

Ticket To _____   It Takes Two To _____

_____ Feeling   _____ Doll

The Magic Of _____   The Reverend And The _____

Songwriters Hall of Fame: Jerry Leiber/Mike Stoller

Hall of Fame Induction: 1985. Just hearing a few Leiber/Stoller song titles help you realize the impact they had on rock and roll in the 50's and 60s. Indeed, they were at the forefront during the birth of rock and roll. Beginning with hits like *Searching* and *Youngblood* by the Coasters and continuing with hits for Elvis like *Hound Dog* and *Jailhouse Rock* the two continued their success in pop music with *Stuck in the Middle With You* for Stealer's Wheel in 1972. **Little known fact:** Leiber and Stoller started their own record label in 1967 devoted to girl groups and hired the songwriting duo of Jeff Barry and Ellie Greenwich. **Recommended listening:** *Leiber & Stoller Present the Spark Records Story, Smokey Joe's Cafe: The Songs of Leiber and Stoller* and *Peggy Lee Sings Leiber & Stoller*.

*"Work like you don't need the money. Love like you've never been hurt. Dance like nobody is watching." -- **Mark Twain***

Inspirational Quote

An Idea to Write a Song About

It's been years since high school and you're looking forward to attending the reunion and seeing all of your old friends. But as you walk in, the first person you see is your old boyfriend/girlfriend.

Note Sequence for a Song
B-G-E-G-B-G-E

Power Words
Cemetery / Parrot / Thunder / Symphony / Frontier

Cliches, Expressions, Slang and Idioms
- There are no words for emptiness
- The bloom is off the rose
- With visions of redemption, I walk against the crowd

Rolling Stone Magazine's Greatest Songs of all Time -- #31
STAIRWAY TO HEAVEN (Led Zeppelin) 1971 (Songwriters: Page/Plant)
A FEW LINES: "There's a lady who's sure. / All that glitters is gold. / And she's buying a stairway to heaven. / When she gets there she knows. / If the stores are all closed. / With a word she can get what she came for. / And she's buying a stairway to heaven."
DID YOU KNOW... *Stairway to Heaven* is one of the biggest-selling sheet music publications in rock history. Since its release in 1971, it has sold more than 1.2 million copies.

Songwriter's Toolkit
Intellitouch Tuners (tuners.com)
This is one of the best electronic tuners on the market. It is designed to tune electric and acoustic guitars, basses, violins, banjos, mandolins and more without interference from ambient room noise, all without the use of wires, microphones or pickups. Tuning in noisy environments is a snap because the unique, flexible clamp actually "feels" the instrument's vibrational energy instead of relying on sound.

Songwriter Quote

"The writing process is never set in cement. You need flexibility." -- *Van Morrison*

SUNDAY

MONDAY

TUESDAY

WEDNESDAY

THURSDAY

FRIDAY

SATURDAY

Songwriting Exercise

Everyone has a favorite television show. Take your favorite show and write a song about it. You can approach this two ways. First you can simply write a song about the show. Many times this can result in a humorous song. Or you can write a song about one of the plot lines changing locations and character names as needed.

Song Titles
- Dreamdance
- Keys To The Coffin
- Hymnasphere
- Bikini Bay In The Middle Of May
- Winking At The Dead

Chord Progression for a Song
C-F-Am-G (I-IV-vi-V)

Word Association Exercises

She Wears Her Love Like _____   _____ River

Who Has The _____   _____ And Ragged

_____ And Bells   _____ Tension

Songwriters Hall of Fame: Bob Gaudio

Hall of Fame Induction: 1995. Bob Gaudio was only 15 years old when he wrote a hit single (*Who Wears Short Shorts?*) for his group, The Royal Teens. But it was his success as the songwriting member of The Four Seasons that gained his ultimate place in songwriting history. He later went on to produce and/or write for Diana Ross, Michael Jackson, Barry Manilow and Neil Diamond. **Little known fact:** Gaudio was producer of the Neil Diamond/Barbra Streisand duet recording, *You Don't Bring Me Flowers*, for which he received a Grammy nomination. **Recommended listening:** *Frankie Valli and the Four Seasons Greatest Hits, Vol. 1, Oh What A Night* and *The Genuine Imitation Life Gazette*.

"There'll be two dates on your tombstone and all your friends will read 'em. But all that's gonna matter is that little dash between 'em..." **-- Kevin Welch**

Inspirational Quote

An Idea to Write a Song About

Write a song about your girlfriend or boyfriend who has one green eye and one blue eye.

Note Sequence for a Song
D-D-D-D-F-E-D

Power Words

Dynamite / Scorpion / Anaconda / Chalet / Gondola

Cliches, Expressions, Slang and Idioms

- It's only fear that makes you stay
- But my intention was good
- It seemed like a good idea at the time

Rolling Stone Magazine's Greatest Songs of all Time -- #32

SYMPATHY FOR THE DEVIL (The Rolling Stones) 1968
(Songwriters: Jagger/Richards)

A FEW LINES: "Just as every cop is a criminal. / And all the sinners saints. / As heads is tails. / Just call me Lucifer. / 'Cause I'm in need of some restraint. / Pleased to meet you. / Hope you guess my name. / But what's puzzling you. / Is the nature of my game."

DID YOU KNOW... The inspiration for this song about the nature of man is said to have come from Soviet writer Mikhail Bulgakov's novel "The Master and Margarita" which depicts Satan having his way in 1930s Moscow.

Songwriter's Toolkit

Songwriting: Essential Guide to Lyric Form and Structure: Tools and Techniques for Writing Better Lyrics (Berklee Press Publications)
by Pat Pattison (ISBN: 0793511801)

Veteran songwriter Pat Pattison's helpful guide contains essential information on lyric structures, timing and placement and exercises to help everyone from beginners to seasoned songwriters say things more effectively and gain a better understanding of their craft. ($16.95)

Songwriter Quote

"It was my 16th birthday - my mom and dad gave me my Goya classical guitar that day. I sat down, wrote this song and I just knew that that was the only thing I could ever really do - write songs and sing them to people." -- Stevie Nicks

SUNDAY

MONDAY

TUESDAY

WEDNESDAY

THURSDAY

FRIDAY

SATURDAY

Songwriting Exercise

Write a song in the first person perspective about an inanimate object. It might be a book. Or perhaps a car. Or even a tea kettle. You can approach this from several directions. You might be a pillow on a bickering couple's bed. You could be a birdhouse providing shelter to a feathered friend. You might even write the song without really saying what you are, but turning it into a musical riddle.

Song Titles

- Where Did I Leave My Shoes?
- Let's Go To The Movie Show
- Reunion
- Do Geeks Wear Glasses Just To Look Smart?
- Heaven Number 7

Chord Progression for a Song
Am-F-E (i-VI-V)

Word Association Exercises

Imaginary _____   Sick As A _____

Midnight In _____   The Wings Of _____

_____ In The Fire   Heavy As A _____

Songwriters Hall of Fame: Holland-Dozier-Holland

Hall of Fame Induction: 1988. Holland-Dozier-Holland is a songwriting and production team comprised of Lamont Dozier and brothers Brian Holland and Edward Holland, Jr.. The trio wrote and arranged many songs which came to be known as the Motown sound in the 1960s. This included 25 Top 10 hits including *Heat Wave* for Martha & the Vandellas, *How Sweet It Is* for Marvin Gaye and many hits for The Four Tops (*Reach Out I'll Be There*) and The Supremes (*Where Did Our Love Go?*). **Little known fact:** Lamont founded The Romeos at the age of 13 and had a charting single with *Fine Fine Baby* on Atco Records in 1957. **Recommended listening:** *Why Can't We Be Lovers: The Invictus Sessions* and *The Picture Never Changes*.

---

*"If you hear a voice within you say 'you cannot paint,' then by all means paint and that voice will be silenced." -- **Vincent Van Gogh***

Inspirational Quote

An Idea to Write a Song About

It may not be the 60's and the heyday of protest songs, but they are still being written. How about *Deja Vu (All Over Again)* from John Fogarty or *Dear Mr. President* by Pink. So write a protest song about something you'd like to see change or improve.

Note Sequence for a Song
G-G-C-B-D-C-B

Power Words
Pearl / Fawn / Fairy / Cobalt / Journey

Cliches, Expressions, Slang and Idioms
• Crying all the way to the bank
• You can't teach an old dog new tricks
• Just catching 40 winks

Rolling Stone Magazine's Greatest Songs of all Time -- #33
RIVER DEEP. MOUNTAIN HIGH (Ike and Tina Turner) 1966
(Songwriters: Spector/Barry/Greenwich)
A FEW LINES: "When you were a young boy, did you have a puppy. / That always followed you around. / Well, I'm gonna be as faithful as that puppy. / No, I'll never let you down."
DID YOU KNOW... Although this song is credited to Ike And Tina Turner, producer Phil Spector forbid Ike to take part in the recording process. Spector wanted his own people to record this and made sure Ike was not in the studio during the sessions.

Songwriter's Toolkit
Music Connection (Published 25 times a year)
Music Connection is considered by some to be the trade publication for the music industry. Each issue contains news items, interviews and articles that relate to and affect the music industry, including columns and guides specifically for musicians and songwriters. ($2.95/single issue or $45/year)

"I remember sitting at a piano and hearing the notes and the chords ring out in the air, and I knew there was something special in that sound, some kind of freedom." -- **Laura Nyro**

SUNDAY

MONDAY

TUESDAY

WEDNESDAY

THURSDAY

FRIDAY

SATURDAY

Songwriting Exercise

Write a song based on a cliche. Now I usually recommend staying away from cliches, but you can't argue with the success many writers have had using them. Check out a book from the library, do an online search or use one included in this book. You'll find dozens of ideas. These are the first three I picked at random. "Survival of the fittest." "Wear out your welcome." "Enemies at the gate." You can imagine a song in every instance.

Song Titles
- A Million And Two
- Queen Of The Rolling Pin
- Dancing In The Dust
- Frankly, My Dear
- Why Can't Happiness Last A Little Longer?

Chord Progression for a Song
C-Am-Dm-G (I-vi-ii-V)

Word Association Exercises

A Breeze As Soft As _____

_____ Heart

_____ And Mountains

High School _____

_____ In America

Sitting Here Thinking Of _____

Songwriters Hall of Fame: Gerry Goffin

Hall of Fame Induction: 1987. Gerry Goffin met Carole King at Queens College and an instant songwriting partnership was born. They were married in 1959 and divorced in 1968, but their songwriting union continued for several more years. He later wrote such hits as *Theme from Mahogany* with Michael Masser for Dianna Ross and *Saving All My Love For You* which assured stardom for Whitney Houston. **Little known fact:** Gerry Goffin was one of the first people to take notice of Kelly Clarkson's talent. He had actually hired her to do demo work prior to her auditioning for and winning the first American Idol title in 2001. **Recommended listening:** *Mahogany* and *Back Room Blood*.

---

*"A painter paints pictures on canvas. But musicians paint their pictures on silence." -- **Leopold Stokowski**

Inspirational Quote

An Idea to Write a Song About
You're a goldfish swimming around in your little goldfish bowl. There are several slants you could take on this. Are you happy and content in your little world or do you actually realize how small it really is?

Note Sequence for a Song
F-F-B♭-A-E-B-C-B-A

Power Words
Parchment / Dagger / Island / Dancer / Dusty

Cliches, Expressions, Slang and Idioms
• All that glitters is not gold
• Behind the clouds, the sun is shining
• Feeling bad is just a new sensation

Rolling Stone Magazine's Greatest Songs of all Time -- #34
YOU'VE LOSE THAT LOVIN' FEELING (The Righteous Brothers)
1964 (Songwriters: Spector/Mann/Weil)
A FEW LINES: "You never close your eyes anymore when I kiss your lips. / There's no tenderness like before in your fingertips. / You're trying hard not to show it, baby. / But baby, baby I know it. / You've lost that lovin' feelin'."
DID YOU KNOW... This is one of the most played songs in radio history and is estimated to have been broadcast over 8 million times to date. A little known fact is that Sonny and Cher were used as back-up singers on the song.

Songwriter's Toolkit
88 Songwriting Wrongs & How to Right Them: Concrete Ways to Improve Your Songwriting and Make Your Songs More Marketable
by Pete Luboff (ISBN: 0898795087)
This unique book covers eighty-eight ways to spot what's wrong with a song - along with expert instruction on how to fix it. Songwriters Pat and Pete Luboff cover it all, pointing out pitfalls and supplying solutions every measure of the way. Writer's Digest Books. ($19.99)

Songwriter Quote

"Traditionally, songwriters can't sing. And that holds true in my case, also." -- John Phillips

SUNDAY

MONDAY

TUESDAY

WEDNESDAY

THURSDAY

FRIDAY

SATURDAY

Songwriting Exercise

This exercise is similar to "random association." (Sometimes this particular exercise is known as "forced association.") Take a sheet of paper and fold it vertically down the center. On the right side jot down 20 nouns. You can do this using free thinking or use a dictionary. Then, making sure the page is folded so you can't see the right hand column, list 20 adjectives. Once you unfold the page see if there are any pairings that beg for you to use in a song. You can do the same thing with verbs and nouns.

Song Titles

- Down By The Dock With Deliah
- Angry Words I Can Never Take Back
- Think Of Me Every Once In Awhile
- Daddy's In The Attic, Momma's In The Cellar
- Scattergun

Chord Progression for a Song
   C-E-Dm-G (I-III-ii-V)

Word Association Exercises

The First Sign Of _____   Born In A _____

Like _____ From Above   The End Of _____

From High Above The _____   There's Nothing Like _____

Songwriters Hall of Fame: Gibb Brothers

Hall of Fame Induction: 1994. Consisting of brothers Barry, Robin and Maurice, the Bee Gees began with hit singles in Australia, but it wasn't long before the trio was known all over the world. They won 9 Grammy awards, have had 5 singles in the Top 10 at the same time and had a string of six #1 singles in a row. They were inducted into the Rock and Roll Hall of Fame in 1997. **Little known fact:** As kids, the brothers were supposed to lip sync to a song at a local cinema. Their record was broken on the way, so they performed live. **Recommended listening:** *Saturday Night Fever Bee Gees' Greatest Hits* and *One Night Only*.

"The power of imagination makes us infinite." -- ***John Muir***

Inspirational Quote

An Idea to Write a Song About

You think you can dance, but you always seem to get strange looks when you're out there on the dance floor. Do you really have two left feet or are people simply jealous. (Think 'Elaine' on *Seinfeld*).

Note Sequence for a Song
C-C-B-B-D-D-A

Power Words

Iceberg / Bounce / Palace / Abstract / Tumbleweed

Cliches, Expressions, Slang and Idioms

- Champagne taste on a beer budget
- Born with a silver spoon in his mouth
- When the pony dies, the ride is over

Rolling Stone Magazine's Greatest Songs of all Time -- #35

LIGHT MY FIRE (The Doors) 1967
(Songwriters: Krieger/Densmore/Morrison/Manzarek)
A FEW LINES: "You know that it would be untrue. / You know that I would be a liar. / If I was to say to you. / Girl we couldn't get much higher. / Come on baby light my fire. / Come on baby light my fire. / Try to set the night on fire."
DID YOU KNOW... The band was asked to change some of the lyrics when they performed on the Ed Sullivan show to make it more "family" suitable. Morrison claims he forgot and performed the song as written. They were subsequently banned from ever playing the Sullivan show again.

Songwriter's Toolkit

Songwriting: And the Creative Process (Sing Out Publications)
by Steve Gillette (ISBN: 1881322033)
Songwriting and the Creative Process provides plenty of information on the nuts and bolts of writing commercially acceptable music. Song structure, rhyme and meter and a good section on hearing musical intervals are included in the book. ($16.95)

Songwriter Quote

*"I think Bridge Over Troubled Water was a very good song. Artie sang it beautifully. The Boxer was a really nice record. But I don't think I've written any great songs." -- **Paul Simon***

SUNDAY

MONDAY

TUESDAY

WEDNESDAY

THURSDAY

FRIDAY

SATURDAY

Songwriting Exercise
Write a song based on a fairy tale. It can either be a favorite fairy tale you remember from your youth or you can even do an internet search and discover a fairy tale you've never heard before. You could use this same concept and write a song based on your favorite Disney animated movie.

Song Titles
- Waiting For A Bus To Anywhere But Here
- Even Killers Have Mothers Who Love Them
- Ghosts I Thought I'd Left Behind
- Baby's Burning Bridges
- I Got Skinned Up Knees From Falling Out Of Trees

Chord Progression for a Song
Am-C-Dm-E (i-III-iv-V)

Word Association Exercises

_____ On The Water   The Wind And The _____

_____ Torture   _____ Nebula

Deep As _____   Standing In The Shadows Of _____

Songwriters Hall of Fame: Isaac Hayes
Hall of Fame Induction: 2005. Isaac Hayes began singing at the age of five at his church and soon after, he taught himself how to play the piano, organ and saxophone. He began his recording career playing saxophone for The Mar-Keys. After writing a string of hit songs at Stax Records with songwriting partner David Porter (including Sam and Dave's *Soul Man* and *Hold On I'm Comin')*, Hayes released his debut album *Presenting Isaac Hayes*. **Little known fact:** Hayes appeared in the 1981 film *Escape from New York* as The Duke of New York. He has appeared in many other films and television shows and also became the first African American to win an Academy Award in a non-acting category for Best Original Song for the film "Shaft." **Recommended listening:** *Isaac Hayes: Greatest Love Songs* and *Hot Buttered Soul.*

---

*"Without music, life would be a mistake." -- **Friedrich Nietzsche***

Inspirational Quote

An Idea to Write a Song About

You fell in love on your first date. You've been waiting patiently near the phone for another call. You haven't slept in nearly two days as you're afraid you might not hear the phone ring. Surely your date felt the same. Didn't they?

Note Sequence for a Song
E-G-E-G-A-E-B-C-B-A

Power Words

Tomb / Satin / Patchwork / Stone / Alien

Cliches, Expressions, Slang and Idioms

- Bags all packed and ready to go
- There is harmony in disharmony
- Another day, another dollar

Rolling Stone Magazine's Greatest Songs of all Time -- #36

ONE (U2) 1992 (Songwriters: Bono/The Edge/Clayton/Mullen)
A FEW LINES: "Did I disappoint you? / Or leave a bad taste in your mouth? / You act like you never had love. / And you want me to go without."
DID YOU KNOW... This is widely considered to be the song that "saved" U2. The band was on the brink of breaking up when they rallied around a riff The Edge was trying to write for the bridge of another composition.

Songwriter's Toolkit

Rhymer (Rhymer.com)
(Online Rhyming Dictionary/Rhyming Software)
You can use a free version of *Rhymer* online or buy an evolved version for your desktop at an affordable price. ($29.99) The desktop version contains a 93,000 word dictionary and can even be used inside Microsoft Word (Windows version). You are able to specify the range of syllables you want, the range of letters you might require and even choose from alternate pronunciations. (e.g., when you type "read" do you want it to sound like "reed" or "red"?) They also offer WriteExpress Phonetic Finder at no cost (Windows only).

"I said, other people can write songs, let's see if I can. So the first 400 or 500 wound up on the floor somewhere." -- Gregg Allman

SUNDAY

MONDAY

TUESDAY

WEDNESDAY

THURSDAY

FRIDAY

SATURDAY

Songwriting Exercise

Take a chord progression of at least 4 chords. (e.g. C-Am-F-G) Now, instead of playing the "standard progression", try mixing the chords up in a different pattern and see what you come up with. Or substitute a chord that normally wouldn't even be used in that particular key.

Song Titles
- Hop, Skip And Jump
- Wounds That Won't Heal
- Is This Town Even On The Map?
- Time Stands Still When She Enters The Room
- Kisses Sweeter Than Turpentine

Chord Progression for a Song
C-B♭-F-G (I-Vii♭-IV-V)

Word Association Exercises

Voice In The _____   _____ In The Dark

Crying For _____   Quick As _____

_____ And The Devil   Mama Told Me _____

Songwriters Hall of Fame: Ashford and Simpson

Hall of Fame Induction: 1988. Although Nickolas Ashford and Valerie Simpson are successful recording artists in their own right, they are probably better known as one of the most successful songwriting teams of the era. (They have also been "successfully" married since 1973.) Dozens of artists have had hits with Ashford-Simpson songs including Marvin Gaye and Tami Terrell (*Ain't No Mountain High Enough*), Aretha Franklin (*Cry Like A Baby*), Gladys Knight (*Didn't You Know You Have to Cry Sometime*), Ray Charles (*Let's Go Get Stoned*) and Chaka Khan (*I'm Every Woman*). **Little known fact:** One of Valerie Simpson's brothers (Raymond) was once a member of the Village People. In 1996, Ashford and Simpson opened a restaurant in New York City called the Sugar Bar. **Recommended listening:** *Is It Still Good To Ya, Stay Free* and *A Musical Affair*.

"I am enough of an artist to draw freely upon my imagination. Imagination is more important than knowledge. Knowledge is limited. Imagination encircles the world." -- Albert Einstein

Inspirational Quote

An Idea to Write a Song About
You are sitting in a dark smoky bar. You begin flirting with someone across the room, but can't really get a good look at them. You finally cross the room only to end up staring across the table at your best friend's beau.

Note Sequence for a Song
G-C-B-C-B-A-G

Power Words
Skyscraper / Dragonfly / Scream / Sparrow / Laughter

Cliches, Expressions, Slang and Idioms
• Behind the clouds, the sun is shining
• When the shoe is on the other foot
• Fancy free

Rolling Stone Magazine's Greatest Songs of all Time -- #37
NO WOMAN, NO CRY (Bob Marley) 1975 (Songwriters: Ford/Marley)
A FEW LINES: "Good friends we have. / Oh, good friends we have lost. / Along the way in this great future. / You can't forget your past. / So dry your tears, I say. / No woman no cry,"
DID YOU KNOW... Marley gave a songwriting credit on *No Woman, No Cry* to childhood friend Vincent "Tata" Ford in order to help keep Ford's Kingston soup kitchen up and running.

Songwriter's Toolkit
My Co-Writer (MyCo-Writer.com)
My Co-Writer is a great tool for songwriters at all levels. The CD includes a collection of 17 original music tracks ready for melody and lyrics. These royalty-free tracks are professionally produced and provide a great foundation for your own composition. It's like having an out-of-town collaborator serving up great songs for you to finish. *My Co-Writer* is a great tool for everyone from novice songwriters to seasoned composers. There are currently 7 different CDs to choose from. ($49.95/each)

Songwriter Quote

"You're taking care of everyday things, but you're living at the edge of a song." -- Laura Nyro

SUNDAY

MONDAY

TUESDAY

WEDNESDAY

THURSDAY

FRIDAY

SATURDAY

Songwriting Exercise

In this exercise you will write the lyrics to your song before you create the melody. For some of you this will seem natural, for others it might seem awkward. (Many songwriters I know feel most comfortable creating lyrics and melodies at the same time.) When you're done writing your lyrics, go back and insert one of the "power words" listed throughout this book to each line of the song. You may end up changing entire lines, but that's fine. I think you'll find the song greatly improved once you are finished.

Song Titles
- Amethyst
- Galleons Of Gold
- Your Eyes Match The Green Of Your Envy
- Miles To Go (But The Tank's On Empty)
- Dreams Of Daytona

Chord Progression for a Song
  C-G-Dm-G (I-V-ii-V)

Word Association Exercises

The Speed Of _____   _____ And Dungeons

_____ In The Sunset   Gold _____

Between A _____ And A _____   Somebody _____ My _____

Songwriters Hall of Fame: Carly Simon

Hall of Fame Induction: 1994. Simon has released over two dozen albums in her career in addition to 13 Top 40 hits on the U.S. charts. She has also written the scores for 4 movies, written 4 children's books and has an opera to her credit. Add to the fact that she has won 2 Grammys, an Emmy and a Golden Globe Award and you can see why she is in the Songwriters Hall of Fame. **Little known fact:** Simon wrote *You're Where I Go* as a tribute to Christa McAuliffe who died in the Space Shuttle Challenger disaster. McAuliffe had a tape of Simon's songs with her that day. **Recommended listening:** *No Secrets, Anticipation* and *Coming Around Again.*

*"Without music, life is a journey through a desert." -- **Pat Conroy***

Inspirational Quote

An Idea to Write a Song About

The odds are it's not Christmas time as you read this, but your assignment is still to write a holiday song. You might be surprised at the need for these types of songs, but dozens of artists release CDs every holiday season.

Note Sequence for a Song
F-F-G-G-A-A-B♭-B♭-A-A-G-A-F

Power Words
Photograph / Nuclear / Vanish / Gold / Voyage

Cliches, Expressions, Slang and Idioms
- A ghost of a chance
- Forever and a day
- Hit me right between the numbers

Rolling Stone Magazine's Greatest Songs of all Time -- #38
GIMME SHELTER (The Rolling Stones) 1969
(Songwriters: Jagger/Richards)
A FEW LINES: "Ooh, a storm is threatening my very life today. / If I don't get some shelter, yeah, I'm gonna fade away. / War, children, its just a shot away, it's just a shot away. / War, children, its just a shot away, it's just a shot away." DID YOU KNOW... Merry Clayton is the female vocalist for the high second vocal track heard in the song. She was a Gospel singer who did backup vocals for various artists including Ray Charles. She later released her own version of this song.

Songwriter's Toolkit
Oasis CD Manufacturing (OasisCD.com) (888) 296-2747
One of the largest and best-known CD duplication companies, Oasis has been serving independent musicians, filmmakers and labels with CD and DVD work since 1987. They offer everything from CD duplication and packaging to promotional tools and distribution. Minimum production numbers for CD runs start at 300 copies.

Songwriter Quote

*"I had to resign myself that I'm not too articulate when it comes to explaining how I feel. But my music does it for me. On the other hand, what I like my music to do is awaken the ghosts inside of me. Not the demons, you understand, but the ghosts." -- **David Bowie***

SUNDAY

MONDAY

TUESDAY

WEDNESDAY

THURSDAY

FRIDAY

SATURDAY

Songwriting Exercise

Write a song with a proper noun in every line of the song. Now the idea here is to still have the song make sense, of course. Using people's names (whether famous, fictional or people you know) will get you part of the way there as will the names of cities, states and countries. As an example, Enya's *Orinco Flow* (often incorrectly referred to as "Sail Away") mentions at least 20 geographical locations in the song. *One Week* by the Barenaked Ladies uses many proper nouns within its unique style.

Song Titles

- Phoebe
- Let's Compromise Over Burgers And Fries
- The Federal Bureau Of Imagination
- Is She Smiling At Me? (Or Is She Just Laughing?)
- Jaguars, Jacuzzis And Jazz

Chord Progression for a Song
C-Bb-F-C (I-VIIb-IV-I)

Word Association Exercises

Buy Me A _____, Please

At The Edge Of _____

Friends I've Never _____

Luck And _____

Like A Common _____

_____ For The Dying

Songwriters Hall of Fame: Van Morrison

Hall of Fame Induction: 2003. The eccentricities of Van Morrison may have kept him from becoming a true pop legend, but his vast group of followers will worship him forever. Born in Belfast, Northern Ireland, his father ardently collected classic American jazz and blues recordings which greatly influenced Morrison musically. He has won four Grammys and was inducted into the Rock and Roll Hall of Fame in 1993. **Little known fact:** Morrison was the lead singer of the Northern Irish band Them and penned their seminal 1965 hit *Gloria*. **Recommended listening:** *Moondance, Wavelength* and *How Long Had This Been Going On.*

"A rock pile ceases to be a rock pile the moment a single man contemplates it, bearing within him the image of a cathedral." -- **Antoine De Saint-Exupery**

Inspirational Quote

An Idea to Write a Song About

We all tell lies, but now you have to admit to telling one in song. Think back on a time you told a big lie. Was it to save the feelings of someone else or to save your own neck? (Remember, no one has to know the song is about you!)

Note Sequence for a Song
F-G#-C-G#-C-G#-F

Power Words
Chameleon / Eagle / Skull / Scribble / Cobblestone

Cliches, Expressions, Slang and Idioms
- Just the tip of the iceberg
- Like a dog lost in high weeds
- Pay as your go

Rolling Stone Magazine's Greatest Songs of all Time -- #39
THAT'LL BE THE DAY (Buddy Holly and the Crickets) 1957 (Songwriters: Allison/Holly/Petty)
A FEW LINES: "Well, when Cupid shot his dart he shot it at your heart. / So if we ever part then I'll leave you. / You sit and hold me and you tell me boldly. / That some day, well I'll be blue."
DID YOU KNOW... The song was inspired by the John Wayne movie *The Searchers* which Holly and group members saw in 1956. Wayne's frequently-used catchphrase, "that'll be the day," inspired the young musicians.

Songwriter's Toolkit
6 Steps to Songwriting Success (Billboard Books)
by Jason Blume (ISBN: 0823084124)
"There are no rules in songwriting," says the author, "but there are 'tools' that can help you achieve your goals." There are reasons why certain melodies stick in your head - and reasons why some lyrics resonate with millions of listeners. This book provides novices an easy to understand, step-by-step approach to mastering those elements consistently found in hit songs. ($21.95).

Songwriter Quote

"All music is folk music. I ain't never heard a horse sing a song." - *- Louis Armstrong*

SUNDAY

MONDAY

TUESDAY

WEDNESDAY

THURSDAY

FRIDAY

SATURDAY

Songwriting Exercise

Go down to your favorite music store or visit *Amazon* or *CD Universe* or *iTunes* and browse through the CD's until you find a CD cover where both the artwork and the CD title grabs your fancy. Think about the artwork and what it conveys as well as the CD title. Then sit down and write a song that conveys what you feel. Even though there are no copyright issues involved, try not to use the CD title as the title of your song. Rather make it more personal so that it expresses the feelings you experienced.

Song Titles
- Green Gardens Growing
- Good Thing There's Only One Of You
- Bad Dreams Lead To Screams
- Cookie Dough Blues
- Bulldogs And Beagles

Chord Progression for a Song
Am-F-D-G (i-VI-IV-VII)

Word Association Exercises

My Kind Of _____   _____ And Dark

_____ And Candy   _____ Fortune

Girls Who Love _____   The Rain Falls Like _____

Songwriters Hall of Fame: Smokey Robinson

Hall of Fame Induction: 1990. Robinson is known to many as "Mr. Motown." It was his acquaintance and work with Barry Gordy Jr. that established the motown sound in the early 1960s. As a member of The Miracles and as a solo artist, Robinson recorded seventy Top 40 hits for Motown between 1959 and 1990. He also wrote hit singles for Mary Wells, the Temptations, Marvin Gaye and The Marvelettes. **Little known fact:** Bob Dylan once described Robinson as "America's greatest living poet." Robinson's songwriting portfolio includes over 4,000 songs. **Recommended listening:** *Being With You, One Heartbeat* and *Warm Thoughts*.

"Success usually comes to those who are too busy to be looking for it." -- Henry David Thoreau

An Idea to Write a Song About

You are booked for a week-long vacation in Jamaica. You haven't had a vacation in two years. But something comes up at work and your boss says he can't do without you. And the weather guy says it's seven below zero...

Note Sequence for a Song
G-C-G-C-E-C-A

Power Words

Darkness / Freedom / Beast / Slash / Goblin

Cliches, Expressions, Slang and Idioms

- Damned if you do and damned if you don't
- An elephant in the room
- Kodak moment

Rolling Stone Magazine's Greatest Songs of all Time -- #40

DANCING IN THE STREET (Martha and the Vandellas) 1964
(Songwriters: Gaye/Hunter/Stevenson)
A FEW LINES: "Calling out around the world. / Are you ready for a brand new beat? / Summer's here and the time is right. / For dancing in the street."
DID YOU KNOW... The interesting loud beat of the drums in the song can be attributed to co-writer Ivy Jo Hunter who banged a crowbar on the concrete floor to add to the existing drum beat track.

Songwriter's Toolkit

Roget A to Z (Collins)
by Robert L. Chapman (ISBN: 0062720597)
For those who prefer a thesaurus in dictionary form, this bestseller is the ideal choice. I use this thesaurus more than the other three versions I have on my desk combined. It is very easy to use and usually gives me more choices than I need. If not, I haul out one of the other three, but don't usually need them. The perfect companion for any songwriter in need of that fleeting word they can't quite grab out of the air. ($15.95)

Songwriter Quote

"The memory of things gone is important to a musician. Things like old folks singing in the moonlight in the back yard on a hot night or something said long ago." **-- Louis Armstrong**

SUNDAY

MONDAY

TUESDAY

WEDNESDAY

THURSDAY

FRIDAY

SATURDAY

Songwriting Exercise

You can do the following exercise several different ways. If you have song-books lying around with songs that you don't know, use them. If not, run out and buy a cheap fake book. (A fake book is a collection of musical lead sheets intended to help a performer quickly learn new songs. Each song in a fake book contains the melody line, basic chords and lyrics.) Using the chords provided (but not the melody line), write a new melody to the chord progression used in one of the songs. Then go back and add your own lyrics.

Song Titles

- Fortune Sometimes Frowns
- Like Diamonds In The Dust
- Greedy Friends
- Heroes And Headlines
- Truckload Full Of Trouble

Chord Progression for a Song
C-G-B♭-F (I-V-VII♭-IV)

Word Association Exercises

Hungry For _____ _____   Sleeping Like A _____

Kisses Like _____   _____ And Moonshine

Twinkle Of An _____   Everytime I _____

Songwriters Hall of Fame: Jim Croce

Hall of Fame Induction: 1990. During his short career, (Croce was killed in a plane crash in 1973 at age 30), Jim Croce released three albums. Eight songs from those albums made the pop charts and 2 of them hit the number one spot (*Bad, Bad Leroy Brown* and *Time In A Bottle*). His last album (*I Got A Name*) was released two weeks after his death. **Little known fact:** Croce earned a degree in psychology from Villanova University and it has been said he had a photographic memory with over 3000 songs in his repertoire. **Recommended listening:** *You Don't Mess Around With Jim, Life & Times* and *I Got A Name*.

"Shoot for the moon. Even if you miss, you'll land among the stars."
-- Les Brown

Inspirational Quote

An Idea to Write a Song About

You were at a bar late last night and when you wake up the next morning you remember this cute guy/girl giving you their phone number. And now you've spent the last four hours frantically trying to find it.

Note Sequence for a Song

A-C-A-C-E-C-B

Power Words

Victorian / Fantasy / Chain / Bedazzle / Prelude

Cliches, Expressions, Slang and Idioms

• Falling through the cracks
• Chapter and verse
• The powers of darkness

Rolling Stone Magazine's Greatest Songs of all Time -- #41

THE WEIGHT (The Band) 1968 (Songwriter: Robbie Robertson)

A FEW LINES: "I pulled in to Nazareth, was feeling 'bout half past dead. / I just need some place where I can lay my head. / Hey mister, can you tell me where a man might find a bed? / He just grinned and shook my hand, "No" was all he said."

DID YOU KNOW... Although Robertson was often seen as the group's de facto leader and was the group's primary songwriter, he sang only a few songs with *The Band*. He later, however, released several solo albums.

Songwriter's Toolkit

How to Write Songs on Guitar: A Guitar-Playing and Songwriting Course by Rikky Rooksby (ISBN: 0879306114)

This book helps transform your guitar-playing skills into creative songwriting techniques. Using well-known songs as examples, plus lots of easy-to-read graphics, the author explains and demonstrates how lyrics, melody, harmony and rhythm work in a song. The straightforward style will have you up and writing on your guitar with ease. ($19.95)

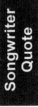

"You've got to create a dream. You've got to uphold the dream. If you can't, go back to the factory or go back to the desk." -- Eric Burdon

SUNDAY

MONDAY

TUESDAY

WEDNESDAY

THURSDAY

FRIDAY

SATURDAY

Songwriting Exercise

Write a children's song. This exercise will actually help strengthen your song-writing skills as you need to keep certain things in mind. For example, you need to keep the chord progression as well as the melody line rather simple. You also need to be repetitive. Many songwriters forget to do this in their songs regardless of their audience. People like to hear the good parts of a song over and over. That's why we have choruses, bridges, hooks and riffs. That doesn't mean your song needs to be boring. Just work harder to make it simple, yet unique.

Song Titles

- If You Haven't Got A Clue, Then Don't Say That You're Trying
- Dream Like A Deadman
- Matthew, Mark, Luke And Juan
- The Monkey Wrote A Classic
- Look! Up In The Sky! (Is That A Pie?)

Chord Progression for a Song
C-Gm-F-C (I-v-IV-I)

Word Association Exercises

Playing Games With _____   Without _____

_____ Clouds   Rythm Of The _____

Glad To Be _____   Too Many _____

Songwriters Hall of Fame: Mac Davis

Hall of Fame Induction: 2006. Mac Davis has had many songs on both the pop and country charts. Many of these were also covered successfully by others. Elvis Presley had several hits singing Davis' tunes including *In The Ghetto* and *Don't Cry Daddy.* Davis was inducted into the Nashville Songwriters Hall of Fame in 2000. He also has television and movie credits to his name. **Little known fact:** Davis has a star on Hollywood Boulevard's Walk of Fame and has a street named after him in his hometown of Lubbock, Texas. **Recommended listening:** *Stop And Smell The Roses, It's Hard To Be Humble* and *Greatest Hits.*

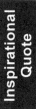

*"Dreams are illustrations from the book your soul is writing about you." -- **Marsha Norman***

An Idea to Write a Song About
Write a song about how one might prepare for a romantic evening. A candle lit dinner at home? A stream of rose petals leading to the bedroom? Tickets to the Chicago Bears' next home game?

Note Sequence for a Song
F-A-C-D-D#-D-C

Power Words
Cool / Prism / Avenue / Mellow / Smoke

Cliches, Expressions, Slang and Idioms
- A little bird told me
- Like a kid in a candy store
- A journey of a thousand miles

Rolling Stone Magazine's Greatest Songs of all Time -- #42
WATERLOO SUNSET (The Kinks) 1968 (Songwriter: Ray Davies)
A FEW LINES: "Dirty old river, must you keep rolling. / Flowing into the night. / People so busy, makes me feel dizzy. / Taxi light shines so bright. / But I don't need no friends. / As long as I gaze on Waterloo sunset. / I am in paradise."
DID YOU KNOW... Ray Davies introduced this to the band while they were in the middle of recording their 5th album. He was reluctant to share the lyrics because they were so personal. He felt "it was like an extract from a diary nobody was allowed to read."

Songwriter's Toolkit
The Complete Rhyming Dictionary (Laurel)
by Clement Wood (ISBN: 0440212057)
This is one of my most frequently used rhyming dictionaries. It is simple to use and should meet the needs of any wordsmith, songwriter or otherwise. It includes over 60,000 entries in all including sight, vowel, consonant, and one-, two-, and three-syllable rhymes. ($7.99)

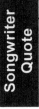
Songwriter Quote

"I wanted to be a secret agent and an astronaut, preferably at the same time." -- David Byrne

SUNDAY

MONDAY

TUESDAY

WEDNESDAY

THURSDAY

FRIDAY

SATURDAY

Songwriting Exercise

Write a song with humor and/or twists. We're not talking about a funny song as there isn't much of a market for those other than children's songs. (Long gone are the days when *Purple People Eater* or *The Monster Mash* could be "monster" hits on the radio.) But use things like irony and paragrams. Use the unexpected. Dylan is famous for lyrics that, well, surprise you. "I thought you'd never say hello... You look like the silent type." Or how about "Her mind is Tiffany-twisted. She got the Mercedes Benz?" from the *Eagles*?

Song Titles

- Girl v2.5
- And The Mind Plays Funny Tricks
- A Light In The Kitchen
- Jubilee
- Anatomy Lessons I'd Love To Learn

Chord Progression for a Song
C-Em-Dm-G (I-iii-ii-V)

Association Exercises

_____ And Pluto

Older Than _____

Driving A Road To _____

_____ Wind

Words That Never _____

Too Tall To Be _____

Songwriters Hall of Fame: Buddy Holly

Hall of Fame Induction: 1986. A young Buddy Holly and his band appeared as an opening act in 1955 for Marty Robbins and a then-unknown Elvis Presley. The band was so impressive it led to Holly's first recording contract. The rest is history including seven Top 40 hits in a two year span. Buddy Holly was also one of the first to use the rock standard of two guitars, a bass and drums in his act. **Little known fact:** Paul McCartney owns the publishing rights to Buddy Holly's song catalog. **Recommended listening:** *That'll Be The Day, Buddy Holly: Greatest Hits* and *'57-'59 Rarities Collection*.

"If there were dreams to sell, what would you buy!" -- ***Thomas Lovell Beddoes***

Inspirational Quote

An Idea to Write a Song About

You are ready to enjoy a nice day off from work. You energetically jump out of bed and dash into the kitchen for some coffee or juice. That's when you spot the list of "things-to-do" your significant other has posted on the fridge.

Note Sequence for a Song
B-B-D#-C#-C#-D-F#-D#-F#-D#-F-D#-B

Power Words
Liberty / Chill / Phantom / Carnival / Silhouette

Cliches, Expressions, Slang and Idioms
- A little of this, a little of that
- Dancing to the beat of a different drum
- Emotional roller coaster

Rolling Stone Magazine's Greatest Songs of all Time -- #43
TUTTI FRUTTI (Little Richard) 1968
(Songwriters: La Bostrie/Penniman/Lubin)
A FEW LINES: "Gotta gal named Sue. / She knows just what to do. / I gotta gal named Sue. / She knows just what to do. / She rocks to the east. / She rocks to the west. / She's the gal that I love best."
DID YOU KNOW... Little Richard sang this during performances as "Tutti Frutti, Good Booty." The song was considered too suggestive for white audiences, so it was cleaned up considerably when he recorded it.

Songwriter's Toolkit
Tascam MFP01 Portastudio
If you're just getting into recording your own music, the MFP01 is the perfect Portastudio for you. Using the MFP01 couldn't be easier ... just pop in a standard cassette tape, plug in your instrument, select the track you want and hit record. You have four tracks to work with, so recording your drum machine, guitar, vocals and keyboard is no problem. If you're a creative musician and want to get into the art of multitrack recording, this is the best place to start. The perfect Portastudio for musicians and novice recordists. ($125.00)

Songwriter Quote

*"But there's nothing that gives me more thrill than when I'm writing and a couplet works. I find the right rhyme, or it's just perfect. There's nothing that exciting." -- **Rosanne Cash***

SUNDAY

MONDAY

TUESDAY

WEDNESDAY

THURSDAY

FRIDAY

SATURDAY

Songwriting Exercise

It's certainly no secret that there have been a lot of songs written about love, but did you know that a recent look at Billboard's Top 5000 hits of the rock era by subject revealed that the number was a staggering 80%? So here's your songwriting exercise for this week. Write a song that is NOT about love in any shape or form. It's not as hard as it sounds, but it will get you out of the norm. Write about a telephone booth or sitting in a traffic jam or standing in line at the grocery store. Your next "love song" can wait another day.

Song Titles

- Antidote To A Love Potion
- Nights In A Soft Pastel
- First Words, Final Words
- Is Your Heart Black Or Just Navy Blue?
- I Hope You Trust The Locksmith

Chord Progression for a Song
Am-F-G-E (i-VI-VII-V)

Word Association Exercises

The Other Side Of _____

Town Without _____

A Touch Of _____

A _____ In The Country

Wild And _____

All About The _____

Songwriters Hall of Fame: James Taylor

Hall of Fame Induction: 2000. If you could look up the phrase singer/songwriter in the dictionary you might very well see a picture of James Taylor. His 1976 album *Greatest Hits* was certified diamond and has sold more than 11 million copies. He has won five Grammy awards including one in 1997 for his *Hourglass* album. **Little known fact:** Taylor had three brothers (Alex, Livingston and Hugh) and a sister (Kate), each of whom released record albums. Children Ben and Sally (both from his marriage with Carly Simon) have also released albums. **Recommended listening:** *Sweet Baby James, October Road* and *Mud Slide Slim and the Blue Horizon.*

"If your dream is big enough, the facts don't count." -- Don Ward

Inspirational Quote

An Idea to Write a Song About
You are running down a dark alley as fast as you can. Sweat is pouring down your face, your legs are aching and you're gasping for breath. But what are you running from?

Note Sequence for a Song
B-D-B-D-E-D-B-D

Power Words
Harbor / Scarab / Glacier / Creature / Bubble

Cliches, Expressions, Slang and Idioms
• A day late and a dollar short
• Even a blind squirrel finds an acorn once in a while
• Preaching to the choir

Rolling Stone Magazine's Greatest Songs of all Time -- #44
GEORGIA ON MY MIND (Ray Charles) 1960
(Songwriters: Carmichael/Gorrell)
A FEW LINES: "Georgia, Georgia, the whole day through. / Just an old sweet song. / Keeps Georgia on my mind. / Talkin' 'bout Georgia. / I'm in Georgia. / A song of you. / Comes as sweet and clear as moonlight through the pines."
DID YOU KNOW... Charles used to sing this as he was being driven about the city. His driver suggested he include it on the album he was working on and the rest is history. In 1979 it became the official song of the state of Georgia.

Songwriter's Toolkit
The Art of Writing Great Lyrics (Allworth Press)
by Pamela Phillips Oland (ISBN: 1581150938)
The author shares a wealth of knowledge about many of the more ambiguous aspects of the field, particularly on how to discriminate lyrics from poetry and how to become an adept observer of everyday conversation. Oland's perspective will intrigue not only followers of the songwriting field but anyone captivated by the art of the written word. ($18.95)

Songwriter Quote

*"I start a lot more songs than I finish, because I realize when I get into them, they're no good. I don't throw them away, I just put them away, store them, get them out of sight." -- **Johnny Cash***

SUNDAY

MONDAY

TUESDAY

WEDNESDAY

THURSDAY

FRIDAY

SATURDAY

Songwriting Exercise

Write a song using the names of colors. We're not looking for a single color here like *Love Is Blue* or *Roses Are Red*. We want you to use as many different names of colors in a song as possible. This is also a great exercise as it helps you focus on power words. What better poetic words are there than azure, burgundy, cobalt or turquoise? Donovan did this especially well with *Wear Your Love Like Heaven* in 1967.

Song Titles

- Got a '52 Chevy And My Foot Is Feelin' Heavy
- Agent Double-Oh-Eleven
- The Hippopotamus Song
- Changing Trains In Trinidad
- Like Paradise On A Sesame Seed Bun

Chord Progression for a Song
C-G-Am-F (I-V-vi-IV)

Word Association Exercises

The Other Side Of _____   A _____ In The Country

Town Without _____   Wild And _____

A Touch Of _____   All About The _____

Songwriters Hall of Fame: John Denver

Hall of Fame Induction: 1996. John Denver had four #1 singles to his songwriting credits not including songs released by other performers. His *Greatest Hits* album ranks as one of the biggest sellers in the history of RCA Records with more than 10 million copies sold. It was Peter, Paul and Mary's #1 hit of *Leavin' On A Jet Plane* which propelled him to stardom. **Little known fact:** Denver won out over 250 applicants when the Chad Mitchell Trio held auditions to replace Mitchell when he left the group. He recorded three albums with the group before moving on to a stellar solo career. **Recommended listening:** *Greatest Hits, Poems, Prayers and Promises* and *Back Home Again.*

Inspirational Quote

"What I like in a good author isn't what he says, but what he whispers." -- **Logan Pearsall Smith**

An Idea to Write a Song About

Are you still living in the town you grew up in? Or have you moved away? What was it like growing up in your hometown? Reflect on these childhood images and put the feelings into song.

Note Sequence for a Song

F-E-D-E-D-G-F-E

Power Words

Wrinkle / Bamboo / Treasure / Pigtails / Windmill

Cliches, Expressions, Slang and Idioms

- Quick and easy
- From here to Timbuktu
- Just a leopard changing spots

Rolling Stone Magazine's Greatest Songs of all Time -- #45

HEARTBREAK HOTEL (Elvis Presley) 1956
(Songwriters: Axton/Durden/Presley)
A FEW LINES: "Since my baby left me. / I've found a new place to dwell. / It's down at the end of Lonely Street. / The Heartbreak Hotel. / I get so lonely. / Baby, you make me so lonely. / I get so lonely I could die."
DID YOU KNOW... This song was co-written by Mae Boren Axton, a teacher in Florida. She was the mother of Hoyt Axton who later wrote such hits as *Greenback Dollar* (The Kingston Trio), *The Pusher* (Steppenwolf) and *Joy to the World* (Three Dog Night).

Songwriter's Toolkit

Epiphone AJ200S Solid-Top Acoustic Guitar
I love Epiphone guitars. I've had the same one for over 40 years and though it doesn't look like much any more, it still sounds great. At under $200, Epiphone offers great value. Unlike many inexpensive guitars, it is very playable. The AJ200S model features a mahogany neck, rosewood fingerboard, body and neck binding and a gently sloped body style that feels great. ($199.95)

Songwriter Quote

"I don't think you get to good writing unless you expose yourself and your feelings. Deep songs don't come from the surface; they come from the deep down. The poetry and the songs that you are suppose to write, I believe are in your heart." **-- Judy Collins**

SUNDAY

MONDAY

TUESDAY

WEDNESDAY

THURSDAY

FRIDAY

SATURDAY

Songwriting Exercise

Write a complete song as quickly as possible, but don't try to rhyme any of the lines as you go. Write 3 or 4 verses plus a chorus. Once you are done you can go back and rework the lines so they rhyme. This is similar to freeform writing except you are writing complete lines and verses, so make the lines flow even if they don't rhyme. Example? "I was sitting at an intersection waiting for the light to change. When I saw this girl/guy walking down the street. They were carrying an umbrella. But I noticed there wasn't a cloud in the sky."

Song Titles

- Stairway To Heaven, Escalator To Hell
- Marching To A Syncopated Beat
- Rusty Memories
- Night Dancing
- The Stars Still Shine In My Half of Heaven

Chord Progression for a Song
C-E-F-D (I-III-IV-II)

Word Association Exercises

Caught In A _____   The Last _____

The Absolute _____   Black And Blue And _____

_____ Night   And It Looks Like _____

Songwriters Hall of Fame: James Brown

Hall of Fame Induction: 2000. "Soul Brother Number One", "The Godfather of Soul", 'The Hardest Working Man in Show Business" and "Mr. Dynamite" are just a few of the titles that James Brown collected over the years. After a brush with the law in the late 40s, Brown joined a musical group called The Flames. They were soon known as James Brown and the Flames and the rest is history. **Little known fact:** Brown had brief stints as a boxer and a baseball pitcher in his career. **Recommended listening:** *Live at the Apollo, In The Jungle Groove* and *The Payback.*

---

*"The art of writing is the art of applying the seat of the pants to the seat of the chair." -- **Mary Heaton Vorse***

Inspirational Quote

An Idea to Write a Song About

It's 2 a.m. You have an important interview in the morning. You've been tossing and turning in bed for hours and just can't seem to get to sleep.

Note Sequence for a Song
E-B-E-B-C-D-C-B

Power Words

Ghost / Kaleidoscope / Hollow / Butterfly / Gangster

Cliches, Expressions, Slang and Idioms

- Quit raining on my parade
- That green-eyed monster called love
- Here's your hat, what's your hurry

Rolling Stone Magazine's Greatest Songs of all Time -- #46

HEROES (David Bowie) 1977 (Songwriters: Bowie/Eno)

A FEW LINES: "I will be king. / And you will be queen. / Though nothing will drive them away. / We can heroes. / Just for one day. / We can be us. / Just for one day."

DID YOU KNOW... Bowie moved to Berlin after becoming burned out from touring. He rented an apartment above an auto-repair shop which is where he wrote this song. Robert Fripp, formerly of King Crimson, played guitar on this.

Songwriter's Toolkit

Rhymesaurus (Purple Room Publishing) PurpleRoom.com

Thesaurus and Rhyming Software for Windows 95/98/ME/NT/2000/XP

Rhymesaurus is the ultimate collection of computer reference software tools for songwriters needing to find just the right word. The rhyming dictionary portion of *Rhymesaurus* contains over 120,000 words and provides 21 different rhyme types including perfect rhymes, reverse rhymes, assonance, consonance and more. It also uses a unique "sounds-like" reference that uses two different algorithms for finding words that sound similar The software also includes Webster's Dictionary and Roget's Thesaurus. ($34.95)

"I think good art happens on that edge between comfortable and in a lot of pain, you know what I mean?" -- **Liz Phair**

SUNDAY

MONDAY

TUESDAY

WEDNESDAY

THURSDAY

FRIDAY

SATURDAY

Songwriting Exercise

Write a song without using a musical instrument. That's right. Put down that guitar or step away from the keyboard. You'd be surprised at how different a song written in this fashion will differ from other tunes you write. The main reason is because you aren't tied to a chord progression or a sequence of notes. One of the best ways to accomplish this (and not be tempted by your favorite instrument) is to go for a nice hike. Set a pace for the beat and start humming or whistling. The physical exercise probably won't hurt you either.

Song Titles

- She Didn't Even Notice I Was Gone
- Just An Old Black Heart
- Feeding Evil Feelings
- Hot As Lightning
- Been Thinkin' 'Bout Thinkin', But Now I'm Just Drinkin'

Chord Progression for a Song
C-Am-F-E (I-vi-IV-III)

Word Association Exercises

_____ Autumn

After The _____

Fine As _____

Searching For _____

Give Me Some _____

Pick Up The Phone And Dial _____

Songwriters Hall of Fame: Bill Withers

Hall of Fame Induction: 2005. Withers might best be known for his #1 hit *Lean On Me* which was inspired by hymns he heard in church growing up and which to this day is still sung in many churches. He also had million-selling singles with classics like *Ain't No Sunshine* and *Just the Two Of Us*. His songs have been used in numerous television commercials and sampled quite often by rap artists. **Little known fact:** Withers spent nine years in the Navy and then worked for Boeing aircraft making toilet seats before hitting the "big time." **Recommended listening:** *Just As I Am, Still Bill* and *Menagerie*.

"All my life I've wanted to be somebody. But I see now I should have been more specific". -- Jane Wagner

Inspirational Quote

An Idea to Write a Song About
You're standing in a field of wildflowers as colorful as a rainbow. They stretch for miles all around you.

Note Sequence for a Song
C-C-D-D#-D#-D-D-D#-F

Power Words
Sparkle / Slippery / Crystal / Viking / Emerald

Cliches, Expressions, Slang and Idioms
• Can't get a word in edgewise
• Gotta get out of Dodge
• The more I learn, the less I know

Rolling Stone Magazine's Greatest Songs of all Time -- #47
BRIDGE OVER TROUBLED WATER (Simon and Garfunkel) 1970
(Songwriter: Paul Simon)
A FEW LINES: "When you're weary, feeling small. / When tears are in your eyes, I'll dry them all. / I'm on your side, oh, when times get rough. / And friends just can't be found. / Like a bridge over troubled water. / I will lay me down."
DID YOU KNOW... When Simon wrote this tribute to friendship, his partnership with Art Garfunkel was nearing an end. (This would be their last album together.) They even disagreed over who should sing it. "He felt I should have done it," Simon later revealed. "And many times I think I'm sorry I didn't."

Songwriter's Toolkit
A Zillion Kajillion Rhymes (Eccentric Software)
This may be the best software rhyming dictionary available. In fact, *The Philadelphia Inquirer* calls it "one of the 6 essential writing tools." The program instantly finds single, double and triple rhymes on literally thousands of words. It claims to find more rhymes than any book in print. You can download a free demo from the Eccentric Software web site. It is limited in scope, but you'll get the idea. ($39.95)

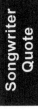

"If it weren't for the rocks in its bed, the stream would have no song." -- Carl Perkins

SUNDAY

MONDAY

TUESDAY

WEDNESDAY

THURSDAY

FRIDAY

SATURDAY

Songwriting Exercise

Using the 5 senses (touch, taste, sound, smell, sight) in songwriting are always important. So let's write a song using every one of the 5 basic senses. You can jump around and use them as you wish or perhaps focus on one of the senses in every verse with the chorus bringing everything back together. It might be a song about love (which might be a bit too easy) or a song about something you treasure. Maybe you're looking through a photograph album and memories of the past come flowing back.

Song Titles

- Love Without Passion Is Like A Car Without Wheels
- Oceans Of Emotion
- Me Likes You
- Double Down And Cross My Fingers
- Violence Fought While Apathy Watched

Chord Progression for a Song
C-F-Am-D (I-IV-vi-II)

Word Association Exercises

Holy _____   Ballad Of The _____

_____ In The Pain   Twenty And _____

_____ In The Basement   In The _____ Of The Moon

Songwriters Hall of Fame: Paul McCartney

Hall of Fame Induction: 1987. Paul McCartney is listed in *The Guinness Book Of Records* as the most successful musician and most successful composer in popular music history with sales of 100 million singles and 60 gold discs. He has released 29 U.S. No. 1 singles, 20 of them with *The Beatles*, the rest with *Wings* and as a solo artist. **Little known fact:** John Lennon met McCartney at a performance in 1957 by John's group, the *Quarrymen*. Impressed by Paul's ability to tune a guitar and his knowledge of song lyrics, John asked him to join the group. **Recommended listening:** *Wings Over America, Tug of War* and *Wingspan: Hits and History*.

"Whether you think you can or think you can't -- you are right." -- *Henry Ford*

Inspirational Quote

An Idea to Write a Song About

Write a song about the age-old story of the devil on one shoulder urging you to do something you shouldn't and an angel on the other telling you not to.

Note Sequence for a Song
D-D#-A-B♭-B♭-C-A-B♭

Power Words

Mushroom / Crosswind / Sanctuary / Tombstone / Arrow

Cliches, Expressions, Slang and Idioms

- Out of the frying pan
- Does the pope wear a funny hat
- Fickle fingers of fate

Rolling Stone Magazine's Greatest Songs of all Time -- #48

All Along The Watchtower (Jimi Hendrix) 1968 (Songwriter: Bob Dylan)

A FEW LINES: "All along the watchtower. / Princes kept the view. / While all the women came and went. / Barefoot servants, too. / Outside in the cold distance. / A wildcat did growl. / Two riders were approaching. / And the wind began to howl."

DID YOU KNOW... Dylan wrote and originally released the song, but it was the Hendrix version that vaulted the number to success. Surprisingly, this was Hendrix's only top 40 hit in the U.S.

Songwriter's Toolkit

How to Be a Hit Songwriter: Polishing and Marketing Your Lyrics and Music (Hal Leonard Corporation)

by Molly-Ann Leikin (ISBN: 063405001X)

You've written what you think is a great melody, what you hope is a strong lyric and you've cut what sounds to you like a killer track. But how do you know if it's a hit? And what do you do with it if it is? One good option is to check out this book which features inside information (including interviews) that can turn your song into a potential hit. ($14.95)

Songwriter Quote

"I wish they'd had electric guitars in cotton fields back in the good old days. A whole lot of things would've been straightened out." -- Jimi Hendrix

SUNDAY

MONDAY

TUESDAY

WEDNESDAY

THURSDAY

FRIDAY

SATURDAY

Songwriting Exercise

This exercise is designed to take you out of your comfort zone. Write a song in someone else's style. (You might even try changing genres.) The best way to accomplish this task is to do a lot of listening first. If you want to emulate Bob Dylan, for example, take the time to listen to several of his songs to get in the right frame of mind. Try and think like he does. Remember, someone like Dylan is a more of a lyricist while even though the *Eagles* have some great lyrics, their melodies are unique and memorable and allow for great harmony.

Song Titles
- Tractors Rusting In The Field
- Got Cold Feet From Standing On The Sun
- I Got A Headache Full Of Love
- Just A Cloudy Disposition
- Things Could Have Turned Out Better (But They Didn't)

Chord Progression for a Song
Am-G-F-Em (I-VII-VI-v)

Word Association Exercises

Ain't It _____

Everybody's Talking About _____

Nothing But _____

Melody For _____

Never Had A _____

Love's Never _____

Songwriters Hall of Fame: Stevie Wonder

Hall of Fame Induction: 1988. No matter what Stevie Wonder wrote about, his songs always had an edge of optimism to them, something few others songwriters manage to do. He has recorded more than 30 top 10 hits, won 21 Grammy awards and has album sales of more than 100 million units. His first album hit the charts in 1963 and over 40 years later he is still releasing highly successfully albums. **Little known fact:** Wonder signed with Motown Records in 1961 (as "Little Stevie Wonder") and remains with the label to this day which is a rarity for any successful artist. **Recommended listening:** *Innervisions, Songs In The Key Of Life* and *Hotter Than July.*

"Most of us go to our grave with our music still inside of us." -- *Anonymous*

Inspirational Quote

An Idea to Write a Song About

Now it's time for a little history for all you younger folk. It's the summer of 1966. Life is pretty good as a 19-year-old hanging around Haight-Ashbury in San Francisco. You thought about going to college, but decided to wait a year or two. The only problem? You just got your draft notice in the morning mail...

Note Sequence for a Song
D-D#-D#-D#-C#-B-B-B

Power Words

Traffic / Slaughter / Pentagram / Dragon / Myth

Cliches, Expressions, Slang and Idioms
- Can't you just read between the lines
- Dogs have masters, cats have staff
- God willing and the creek don't rise

Rolling Stone Magazine's Greatest Songs of all Time -- #49

HOTEL CALIFORNIA (The Eagles) 1976
(Songwriters: Felder/Frey/Henley)
A FEW LINES: "Last thing I remember, I was running for the door. / I had to find the passage back to the place I was before. / 'Relax,' said the night man, 'We are programmed to receive. / You can checkout any time you like. / but you can never leave!'"
DID YOU KNOW... Although the song won the 1977 Grammy for Record Of The Year, members of the band did not show up to accept the award as Don Henley did not believe in contests.

Songwriter's Toolkit

John Pearse Strings (jpstrings.com)
I have used nothing but John Pearse guitar strings for over two decades and have only been tempted once or twice to try a "new and better" string. Every single time I switched back to Pearse strings. Not only do they seem to last longer than other strings, they retain great tonal quality over time as well. Their Phosphor Bronze Extra Lights make any guitar easier to play.

"A lot of songs you write are just for exercise - just pencil sharpeners." -- Harlan Howard

SUNDAY

MONDAY

TUESDAY

WEDNESDAY

THURSDAY

FRIDAY

SATURDAY

Songwriting Exercise

This exercise shows how the key you choose affects the melody of the song. First write the lyrics to a verse. Now, beginning in the key of A, write a melody to those words. Now move to the key of B and create a different melody to the same lyrics. Move on through the major scales until you have 7 somewhat different tunes. Does one stick out from the pack? Writing in one key or another will usually lead to different chord progressions and melodies based, for the most part, on your vocal range.

Song Titles

- I Believe In Love And Laughter
- Ghostwind
- A Critical Level Of Loneliness
- Brick By Brick
- Eagles Don't Fly, They Soar

Chord Progression for a Song
C-Dm-Am-Em (I-ii-vi-iii)

Word Association Exercises

Blonde _____   Bells And _____

Down By The _____   Walking By The _____

_____ Village   Whispers In The _____

Songwriters Hall of Fame: Mick Jagger/Keith Richards

Hall of Fame Induction: 1993. Next to the songwriting team of Lennon/McCartney, the Jagger/Richards duo may be the most famous songwriting team in rock history. Under their leadership, the *Rolling Stones* have had nine #1 albums and over 40 songs in the Billboard Top 40 with eight singles reaching the #1 spot. They were inducted into the Rock and Roll Hall of Fame in 1989. **Little known fact:** The group's second single, *I Wanna Be Your Man,* was given to them by the Lennon/McCartney songwriting tandem. **Recommended listening:** *Sticky Fingers, Let It Bleed* and *Voodoo Lounge.*

*"Music is what feelings sound like." -- **Author Unknown***

Inspirational Quote

An Idea to Write a Song About

You wake up one morning and discover that you don't have a penny to your name. However, you suddenly realize you feel extremely happy.

Note Sequence for a Song
E-B-B-B-A-B-G-A

Power Words

Fleabag / Velvet / Vulture / Umbrella / Shotgun

Cliches, Expressions, Slang and Idioms

- Don't shoot me, I'm just the messenger
- Just going through the motions
- Chasing two rabbits

Rolling Stone Magazine's Greatest Songs of all Time -- #50

THE TRACKS OF MY TEARS (Smokey Robinson and The Miracles) 1965 (Songwriter: Moore/Robinson/Tamplin)

A FEW LINES: "So take a good look at my face. / You'll see my smile looks out of place. / If you look closer, it's easy to trace. / The tracks of my tears."
DID YOU KNOW... Pete Townshend became obsessed with the way Robinson put across the word substitute in the song ("Although she may be cute/She's just a substitute"). It is, in fact, how he came to write the Who's 1966 hit *Substitute*.

Songwriter's Toolkit

MasterWriter (MasterWriter.com)

This software program for Windows and Mac doesn't come cheap at over $200, but it might be the most complete collection of songwriting tools available. It includes a rhyming dictionary, a dictionary containing phrases, cliches and word combinations, a rhymed-phrases dictionary with over 36,000 entries, an alliterations dictionary, the American Heritage Dictionary and Roget's II Thesaurus, a state-of-the-art database that allows you to keep track of all the lyrics, melodies and information related to your songs, a stereo hard disk recorder for recording your ideas and much more. ($228.00)

Songwriter Quote

"I talk to people who are musicians, and they go, Oh this is hell. And I go, Are you kidding me? You never put tar paper on a roof, did ya?" -- Chris Isaak

SUNDAY

MONDAY

TUESDAY

WEDNESDAY

THURSDAY

FRIDAY

SATURDAY

Songwriting Exercise

Most of us are songwriters and not composers. (There is a difference you know.) And even though some of us listen to classical music now and then, we don't relate to it once we go back to our guitar or keyboard. So in this exercise you need to spend at least an hour listening to some classical music. Hopefully you have some in your music collection, but if not there are online resources for accomplishing this. Once your hour is up, try to write something from the mood that has been created.

Song Titles
- Backyard Baseball
- Buenos Noches And Good Night
- Tower Of Babble
- Back When Hip Hop Was What Rabbits Did
- Ceremony

Chord Progression for a Song
C-E-F-G (I-III-IV-V)

Word Association Exercises

_____ Frogs   Rich As A _____

Sharing _____   _____ Of The Song

Living In A _____   _____ And Music

Songwriters Hall of Fame: John Lennon

Hall of Fame Induction: 1987. Perhaps not recognized as much for his post-Beatles years as much as Paul McCartney, Lennon was still one of the prime songwriters of his time whether it was with the Beatles or as a solo artist. Of course, we must also recognize the fact that his life was cut short by his death in 1980. His 1971 song *Imagine* is still considered one of the greatest songs of all time. **Little known fact:** Lennon was given the middle name "Winston" after Britain's prime minister at the time. He later changed it to "Ono." **Recommended listening:** *Imagine, Walls and Bridges* and *Double Fantasy.*

"You are the music while the music lasts." -- T.S. Eliot

Inspirational Quote

An Idea to Write a Song About

You are on a romantic date with your new beau when you find yourself sitting at a table right next to your old beau.

Note Sequence for a Song
G-B♭-C-D-C-C-D-C-B♭-G

Power Words

Tower / Cathedral / Chateau / Rainfall / Dreamer

Cliches, Expressions, Slang and Idioms

- There's no trouble like old trouble
- Get your ducks in a row
- On a wing and a prayer

Rolling Stone Magazine's Greatest Songs of all Time -- #51

THE MESSAGE (Grandmaster Flash and the Furious Five) 1982
(Songwriters: Bootee/Mel)

A FEW LINES: "Don't push me, cause I'm close to the edge. / I'm trying not to loose my head. / It's like a jungle sometimes, it makes me wonder. / How I keep from going under."

DID YOU KNOW... *The Message* was one of 50 recordings chosen in 2003 by the Library of Congress to be added to the National Recording Registry.

Songwriter's Toolkit

TAXI (www.taxi.com) 1-800-458-2111

If you're a songwriter, moving to Los Angeles, New York or Nashville and "paying your dues" might seem like the best way to go. But can you just walk away from your life, your job and your family? What you really need is a vehicle to help you get your music to the right people. TAXI is the world's leading Independent Artist & Repertoire Company, specializing in giving songwriters real access to the people in the music business who have the power to sign deals. The cost to join is a little pricey, but if you're a songwriter trying to get your music before the people that count, TAXI is definitely worth a look.

Songwriter Quote

"I think if you are writing an instrumental you are dealing with more of an aesthetic in a sense, but a lyric is more of a putting yourself on the line and a much more expensive exercise." -- ***Leo Kottke***

SUNDAY

MONDAY

TUESDAY

WEDNESDAY

THURSDAY

FRIDAY

SATURDAY

Songwriting Exercise

Here's an exercise that will probably bring about feelings you normally might not incorporate into a song. Go into your living room or den and look around. Study the items around the room. The artwork, the nic nacs, even the carpet and drapes. What feelings do they convey? Will your song be about comfort and happiness or about four walls with nothing on them and an orange crate for a coffee table? Either way, you have the makings of a song all around you.

Song Titles

- The Elf's on the Shelf, But the Gnome Went Home
- A Twist of Hate
- How Could You Get Lost In Lubbock?
- Feel Like Floating
- A White House On Main Street

Chord Progression for a Song
C-Em-Am-G (I-iii-vi-V)

Word Association Exercises

There's A _____ In My _____   The Lights Of _____

_____ Smiles   _____ In Flight

The Gates Of _____   _____ Stranger

Songwriters Hall of Fame: Bobby Darin

Hall of Fame Induction: 1999. Although most people recognize Bobby Darin as a performing artist, he was one of the earliest examples of the singer/songwriter genre. In fact, he penned two of his earliest hits: *Splish Splash* and *Dream Lover*. He eventually became one of the hottest nightclub performers around, setting attendance records at the famed Copacabana nightclub. **Little known fact:** Darin actually shared songwriting credits on *Splish Splash* with disc jockey Murray the K who bet Darin he couldn't write a song that began with the words "Splish, splash, I was taking a bath." **Recommended listening:** *Darin At The Copa*, *You're The Reason I'm Living* and *If I Were A Carpenter*.

*"Hide not your talents, they for use were made, what's a sundial in the shade?" -- **Benjamin Franklin***

Inspirational Quote

An Idea to Write a Song About
You meet a girl/guy at a party and have a great night. You set up another date, but when you drive up to the address they gave you, you discover they live in a) a mansion or b) an old tenement.

Note Sequence for a Song
C-D#-D#-F-F-F#-F-C-D#-C

Power Words
Maze / Arabesque / Locomotive / Promenade / Lavender

Cliches, Expressions, Slang and Idioms
• Same old song and dance
• Blowing out the candles
• One in a million

Rolling Stone Magazine's Greatest Songs of all Time -- #52
WHEN DOVES CRY (Prince) 1994 (Songwriter:Prince)
A FEW LINES: "Maybe I'm just like my father - 2 bold. / Maybe U're just like my mother. / She's never satisfied. / Why do we scream at each other? / This is what it sounds like when doves cry."
DID YOU KNOW... Although Prince's drummer and bass player from his band, The Revolution, appear to play in the video version of the song, there is no bass in the song and the percussion track was played by drum machine.

Songwriter's Toolkit
Finale SongWriter (Make Music)
While *Finale SongWriter* makes it easy to create great sheet music at an affordable price, that's just the beginning. This program for PC or Mac allows you to enter notes from a mouse, computer keyboard or midi keyboard. You can also add chord symbols, fret board diagrams and multiple verses of lyrics as well as automatically add two and three voice harmony or instantly add a drum part. If getting music on the printed page is part of your songwriting project, *Finale SongWriter* is the perfect collaborator. ($49.99)

Songwriter Quote

"I believe in everything until it's disproved. So I believe in fairies, the myths, dragons. It all exists, even if it's in your mind. Who's to say that dreams and nightmares aren't as real as the here and now?"
-- John Lennon

CPSIA information can be obtained at www.ICGtesting.com
Printed in the USA
LVOW03s1818300514

387964LV00023B/518/P

9 780978 792510